Artist: Francine Auger

William Lyon Mackenzie King, 187·

lian goodall

lian goodall likes to wear many different professional "hats." She has worked as a classroom and museum educator. At present she is a children's book reviewer, author, editor, historical researcher, and performer. She first became fascinated with William Lyon Mackenzie King's story while she was working as a bilingual historic interpreter at King's boyhood home, Woodside National Historic Site of Canada in Kitchener, Ontario.

lian was born in St. Catharines, grew up in Fergus, Ontario, and has lived in France. Currently she lives in Ottawa, just around the corner from Laurier House, King's Ottawa residence. She walks past Laurier House every day and wonders where Pat, King's Irish terrier, used to bury his bones. To find out more about lian's first book on Argentine soccer star Diego Maradona or her current projects, go to her Web site at www.liangoodall.com.

William Lyon Mackenzie King

Canadian Cataloguing in Publication Data

Goodall, Lian

William Lyon Mackenzie King: dreams and shadows

(The Quest Library ; 19).
Includes bibliographical references and index.

ISBN 1-894852-02-8

1. King, William Lyon Mackenzie, 1874-1950. 2. Canada – Politics and government – 1921-1930. 3. Canada – Politics and government – 1935-1948. 4. Prime ministers – Canada – Biography. I. Title. II. Series: Quest Library; 19.

FC581.K5G66 2003   971.062'2'092   C2003-940264-9
F1033.G66 2003

Legal Deposit: Second quarter 2003
National Library of Canada
Bibliothèque nationale du Québec

XYZ Publishing acknowledges the support of The Quest Library project by the Canadian Studies Program and the Book Publishing Industry Development Program (BPIDP) of the Department of Canadian Heritage. The opinions expressed do not necessarily reflect the views of the Government of Canada.

The publishers further acknowledge the financial support our publishing program receives from The Canada Council for the Arts, the ministère de la Culture et des Communications du Québec, and the Société de développement des entreprises culturelles.

Chronology: Lynne Bowen
Index: Darcy Dunton
Layout: Édiscript enr.
Cover design: Zirval Design
Cover illustration: Francine Auger
Photo research: lian goodall

Printed and bound in Canada

XYZ Publishing
1781 Saint Hubert Street
Montreal, Quebec   H2L 3Z1
Tel: (514) 525-2170
Fax: (514) 525-7537
E-mail: info@xyzedit.qc.ca
Web site: www.xyzedit.qc.ca

Distributed by: Fitzhenry & Whiteside
195 Allstate Parkway
Markham, ON L3R 4T8
Customer Service, tel: (905) 477-9700
Toll free ordering, tel: 1-800-387-9776
Fax: 1-800-260-9777
E-mail: bookinfo@fitzhenry.ca

Mackenzie KING

William Lyon

DREAMS AND SHADOWS

XYZ
Publishing

To two women, who dreamed and worked past what their bodies would easily allow them to do. Their examples gave me the inspiration to complete this work: Cathy Pyke, a determined fighter who came back from near death, and Jean Hutchinson (1910-1997), who wrote her history books, even while ill in bed, by tapping on an electric typewriter with two pencils to accommodate her arthritis.

Contents

Grandfather.
William Lyon Mackenzie.

Mother.
Isabel Mackenzie King.

Father.
John King, K.C.

Prologue

Laurier House, Ottawa
December 17, 1943

> Best wishes on your birthday and God bless
> you and keep you in the best of health for
> your benefit and for the nations that have
> already benefitted where your name is writ-
> ten in their hearts and on their minds forever.
> One of your loyal friends,
> Mrs. Mabel Carlesso

Prime Minister William Lyon Mackenzie King felt
humbled to receive such a wonderful card for his
sixty-ninth birthday. It was a moving tribute, a simple
manifestation of trust. Yet, guiding the people of
Canada so often felt like a burden, especially since the
beginning of the war. With Christmas drawing nearer,
King thought of the fighting men. His own nephew,
Lyon King, had been killed, and King shuddered to
think that many men might meet a similar fate. War
raged abroad, but at home, English Canadians clam-
oured for overseas conscription while the people of
Quebec were so strongly opposed to it that King feared
civil war might befall his beloved country. Although he
sometimes felt unsure and alone in the position of

prime minister, King knew he had guidance. He felt those he loved, and who had left this earth, were still near him, assuring him that he was doing the will of God.

His life's work was to help people. King put the flowered birthday card away and called for the dispatches. It was time to start his work for the day. It was time to address the problems of the Dominion of Canada, and indeed, the world.

But before King settled into reading the official documents before him, one of his secretaries, Dr. James Gibson, couldn't help noticing the prime minister "beamed just a little."

It was, after all, his birthday.

1

Nest of Dreams

17. December, die Frau von John King in Berlin,
einen Sohn.

Berlin, now known as Kitchener, was in 1874 a town
of 3,000 in Southern Ontario. It had such a large
Mennonite population that the *Berliner*, John's uncle's
newspaper, announced the news in German. The birth
announcement read: 17. December, to the wife of John
King in Berlin, a son.

John King almost missed the event.

That day, John was dreaming of moving towards a
brighter world. The elders of society might be nodding
off to memories of the glory of the British Empire, but
King was seated at a meeting, listening intently to a

Woodside, happy home of Willie, old Bill the horse, Bella, mother Isabel (seated), Jennie, Max (seated), and Fanny (who is hiding under the table).

Reform Association speech. At a burst of applause, John spoke excitedly to the man beside him. "This man is a friend to liberty!"

A lawyer, newspaperman, and active Liberal politician, King admired reformers such as the speaker. He also held his wife's father, William Lyon Mackenzie, in great esteem. Some people referred sneeringly to the leader of the Upper Canadian Rebellion of 1837 as a notorious rebel who had incited the people. King felt, however, Mackenzie was an example of those who fought for justice. As a newspaperman, mayor of York (which became Toronto), and a member of the Legislative Assembly, Mackenzie had witnessed the actions of the British government, which he felt were unfair in dealing with the people of the colony. He saw his fellow men as enslaved and oppressed at the hands of a few privileged people he dubbed the "Family Compact." As an editor and politician he first tried to make changes peacefully, but by 1837 the time to seek reform quietly had passed. In 1837 Mackenzie urged armed action – rebellion!

By 1874 Mackenzie had been dead for more than a dozen years. Although his brave attempt had failed, many of the reforms he believed in had come to pass. John King's generation enjoyed the benefits of being able to vote for responsible government, but as the speaker that day pointed out, there were the issues that still required change. King himself might put up his fists to defend his personal honour, but he wasn't such a hothead that he charged about with mobs waving pikes and pitchforks. After all, he and his wife were expecting their first child, William Lyon Mackenzie's grandchild.

Before King could settle into listening again, he felt an urgent tapping on his shoulder.

"Mr. King, a message. It's your wife. They've already sent for the doctor."

John stood up, half knocking over his chair. Something was very wrong. Isabel was not expected to have the baby for another month. He needed to be back at Benton Street as fast as a horse could get him there.

John and Isabel already had a beautiful year-old daughter, Isabel or Bella. Bella had gone to John's Uncle Dougall Macdougall's house. There she would stay with her Grandmamma, John's mother, Christina King, and his Aunt Flora. John was free to do a lot of pacing and hand wringing. It was a cold night. Fetching wood and stoking the fire in the wood stove kept him busy.

Finally, in the early hours of the morning, Dr. Bowlby appeared in the bedroom door holding a bundle. "I'd like to announce the safe arrival of a baby boy!" he trumpeted. "Mother and baby are doing well." The doctor neared the wood stove and unfolded a corner of the blanket.

King peered at the red, scrunchy face of his newborn son. "Well, well, well," he admired. "I have decided," he told his wee lad softly, "and your mother agreed, that we shall call you William Lyon Mackenzie." He glanced at Bowlby, his eyes twinkling merrily. "William Lyon Mackenzie King has a nice ring to it, an important ring, don't you think?" And then he answered himself, "Why yes, it does."

∞

Although he had been born prematurely, baby Willie thrived. Soon he was toddling about the house, chasing the cat and trying to mount his big wooden rocking horse by himself. His mother thought he looked simply cherubic. His innocent blue eyes were full of curiosity, his blond hair curled sweetly around his chubby face, and his plump little legs peeked out like German sausages from under his dress, the garb for both boys and girls of the day.

Two years later there was another baby in the family, when Janet (known as Jennie) arrived in 1876. During her pregnancies and confinements, Isabel might not always feel like romping across the carpet with her children and roaring like a lion. A nurse-maid helped her with the children's care, but their mother was always available for merriment! After dinner she played the piano and sang hymns and other songs. Sometimes John joined in and even accompanied her with clacking castanets. The little family had a lot of fun before quieting down later each evening to games and stories read aloud. As both John and Isabel King were of Scottish ancestry and very devout Presbyterians, they would read the bible and hear the children say their prayers every night before they went to bed.

∞

Willie awoke to the sound of little Jennie's crying. He couldn't get back to sleep.

"Tell me the grandfather story," he demanded of his mother as she perched on the edge of his bed.

"*Which* grandfather story?" Isabel queried, tucking the coverlet around Willie's small frame. "You have two grandfathers, young lad. Both came from Scotland and both were very brave and important men, like you shall be one day. Would you like to hear about Father's father, Bombardier King? At the Battle of the Windmill the Royal Artillery fought off the Rebel sympathizers!"

"No, not that grandfather – *my* grandfather," the little boy insisted. He didn't mean any disrespect toward his soldier grandfather who had fought against the other grandfather's forces. But Willie wanted to hear about the person for whom *he* was named.

"Oh!" Isabel chuckled. So her father's exploits had become *the* story.

"My father, William Lyon Mackenzie, was a man with strong ideas who wanted to help people." In the lamplight she wove a story of good and evil – the brave farmers and their leader against the government and its selfish, powerful friends. "Grandfather felt he had to take more action than writing or editing a newspaper or even than he could when he had been mayor of York." Isabel's account contained many exciting details – but Willie liked best the part *after* the Rebel forces lost the battle. He was thrilled each time he heard Isabel tell about the daring escape through the countryside "just a few miles from here. There was a large reward offered for Grandfather's capture, one thousand pounds to any one who would 'apprehend and deliver' him. You've seen the very poster that many greedy men also saw that day. However, a good man and lover of reform posted scouts, who found Grandfather before his enemies did. They took him across the Grand River and gave him shelter for the night. The next day they sent him on his way to safety across the border to Buffalo. Grandfather never forgot their kindness."

Although she made her father's life sound like an adventure story, Isabel couldn't help adding her own personal colouring in a quieter voice.

"I was born the same year as your father, in 1843. Only I was born in the United States, after Grandmother Isabel, who is an angel now, joined Grandfather in New York State. I was the youngest of thirteen children, although not all survived. Things were very difficult." She told Willie of the hardships she had known, how her father was often without work, and once even imprisoned for breach of the American neutrality laws! Her life continued to be difficult and some people snubbed them, even after a pardon permitted the family to return to York. When her father died in 1861, they had bravely struggled on. "Then your Uncle Charles Lindsey introduced me to a good and handsome student from the University of Toronto – but now we're getting into another story and it's time for you to go back to sleep!"

She smoothed his hair and kissed his face tenderly before she took the lamp and left the room.

∞

The importance of family traditions is reflected in the names the Kings gave their four children. The first baby girl was named Isabel Christina Grace, after her mother and grandmothers. The second child, the couple's first born son, was given the name of Isabel's father, William Lyon Mackenzie. Their third child, a daughter, was Janet Lindsey (but called Jennie). Her namesake was her mother's sister, Aunt Janet, who had married Charles Lindsey. When the fourth and last King child was born in 1878, he was given the name of John's uncle, Dougall Macdougall. The young Dougall Macdougall, however, would be always known as Mac or Max.

John and Isabel had grown up in an age when it was expected that families would help each other. In the days before government programs provided any help, it was common for elderly or widowed people to be looked after by their family. John King's father had died before he was born, so he and his mother had lived with his uncle, Dougall Macdougall, a Berlin newspaper editor.

When John finished school, he returned to Berlin and opened his law practice. He and Isabel had a long courtship, but John wasn't established enough to marry her and bring her from Toronto to Berlin until 1872. Like most parents, John and Isabel created hopes and dreams for the four precious children they had. They wanted their offspring to be respected people and important citizens – the girls to have secure marriages and the boys to have important careers. Helping their children achieve these goals meant sacrifices. True, John King wanted to make the world a better place, but his first commitment was to see that his children had education, connections, and opportunities to ensure their success. The Kings did much more than provide food and shelter for their family. They opened doors to their children's futures by exposing them to important people and ideas – even when they were very young.

∽

The crowd pressing around Willie made him hot in his suit jacket and woollen knickers. He squeezed his father's hand for reassurance. John smiled at his seven-year-old son. "Can you see?" he asked. When the lad shook his head "no," John lifted him up.

Now Willie could see the speaker on the platform. The tall, dark-haired man with a funny nose, Willie knew, was Prime Minister Sir John A. Macdonald, the most important person in Canada. That was why his father had brought him to the meeting.

"I would like to thank you," Macdonald concluded. The audience clapped, Willie very enthusiastically.

A young woman crossed the stage, curtsied, and held out a posy. The prime minister bent to receive the flowers, and the giver innocently placed a kiss on his cheek. Macdonald was enchanted. So was Willie. He would never remember what it was that Macdonald had said, but he would never forget the charming rewards that political greatness could hold.

∽

Willie enjoyed the benefits of having parents who were well known in Berlin, but he was not growing up in a rich family. The Kings' bills exceeded John's income. However, while John and Isabel did not belong to the upper classes, they wanted to *appear* to be people of means. Even though John would never own a home, the Kings felt they should live in a place that would impress their friends and potential clients. They needed enough room for their children, their visitors, the family members who stayed with them, and the servants they often employed. In 1886, when Bella was twelve, Willie eleven, Jennie nine, and Max seven, the family rented the last home they would live in in Berlin – Woodside. They would remember it as a warm nest where they had their best family times.

Woodside was a golden-bricked showpiece just outside of town, with over five and a half wooded hectares for enjoying the pleasures of Nature. There were flower gardens to dream in; Lovers' Lane for rambles; a lily pond for reflecting; a hilltop above the orchard where the children could camp; shady nooks for sharing books of poetry, and woodsy knolls, where on sunny days, Isabel could set up her easel and paint.

Inside, Isabel began decorating and remodelling. The Kings were usually able to hire a man and a woman to help Isabel and the children with the many indoor and outdoor duties. The family still had time for a whirl-wind of activities and often went out – skating, sleighing, curling, camping, or attending teas, concerts, church events, and meetings. Between the gay parties at Woodside and the busy schedule away from home, the Kings' social lives sparkled with laughter and friendship.

The happy mood was tempered with duty. In addition to the gardening, cleaning, and other chores, the four King children were expected to devote themselves to the tasks of intellectual preparation. Schoolwork did not stop even after several hours of homework. John King hired a governess to assist the children with German and other subjects. Many Berliners were more fluent in German than in English. When Miss Siebert came to stay with the family, the local Presbyterian minister and family friend, Reverend Mr. Winchester, was also included in the little Woodside German classes.

When their noses weren't in school books, the Kings were always reading something else. Almost every evening the cozy panelled library was alive with discussions regarding events they had read about in newspapers or the books that lined the walls. Reading and thinking about important issues was part of the children's heritage. Grandfather Mackenzie and Great-Uncle Macdougall had edited newspapers. Their father not only wrote articles for newspapers and other publications, but also legally represented the Canadian Press Association. At Woodside, John wrote a book about his father-in-law, in which he argued that Mackenzie was a misunderstood man. The King children were encouraged to have their own opinions, and to seek to do good, to make Berlin and the world beyond a better place.

∞

The students in the gymnasium of the Berlin High School were beginning to squirm, and Willie couldn't help but notice. Most times he'd rather be having fun by joining his classmates on the cricket or football field or engaging in some silly prank. But today he wanted them to listen. He was speaking about something important.

"The next topic addressed," King began, assailing a fresh section of his lengthy speech, "concerned... "

"Mr. King," Principal Connor was on his feet. He peered at Willie over his pince-nez glasses, and his flowing white beard touched his chest as he tilted his head. "We must proceed with the other items on our agenda. I would like to thank you for your interesting narrative on the political meeting you attended." Willie took his seat to the sound of his classmates' applause.

"That's my brother, Old Grandpa," Bella whispered to her seatmate, Emma Bauer.

"Old Grandpa?" the girl whispered back. "Is that because he's named after his grandfather?"

"That and because he's as serious as a little old man, always setting us on the *right* path" his sister replied.

"I think," Zulema Seyler piped up, "that Willie King is a silver-tongued orator." Her friends giggled.

"He may want to be a politician one day," his friend Oscar Rumpal contributed," but if you meet Billy in a fist fight you'll know why we call him The Rebel."

"Young ladies *and* gentleman!" a teacher reproached sternly.

☙

John King's Law Office, Germania Block
Berlin, Ontario
August 6, 1888

"May I help you?" The young man looked up with serious blue eyes. As the teenager was costumed in a suit and tie, despite the August heat, the messenger assumed he was the office clerk.

"Give this bill for telegramming to Mr. King, will you?"

"Mr. King is in Muskoka, vacationing."

"Vacationing, eh? That might explain why he hasn't paid it yet. When's he back?"

"Tuesday next."

"Just give it to him then."

"I will direct it to his attention immediately upon his return," William smiled confidently.

The man left and Willie set the bill on the pile of invoices growing between the stacks of newspaper clippings and letters on the desk. Next to the telephone he had cleared a space and was writing a letter. At age fourteen, Willie increasingly took on more responsibilities in his role of the eldest son. He kept an eye out for his siblings, helped his parents, and even minded his father's business.

He reread the paragraphs he had written under John King's letterhead.

"Dear Papa and Mama," he had begun, "I must answer your loving letter..." He followed with a report of duties as the man in charge.

I have protested two notes and while I was at the bank yesterday there were two notes but

the one was recalled... Bella was at a small
party for tea at Clara Simpson's last night and
enjoyed herself very much. There were only
girls invited. I couldn't say that Robert has
done much work lately excepting talking and
watching us play. Mary is a little cross to us...
nevertheless we are getting along first rate...

Satisfied, he dipped his pen in the ink. It was time
to get to the heart of the matter.

I can just imagine you sitting there, Papa
reading the letters and Mamma sitting listening to them with eager eyes and both of your
hearts full. For I know that mine was when I
got your letter and you saying what a brutal
thing it was for any person to poison our dear
little Fanny.

Willie felt a stab of pain as he remembered their
dear, loving black dog, Fanny. He had been the one to
receive the news from the hired man that their pet had
been found dead, poisoned. Though he thought his
heart would break from grief and shock, he had been
obliged to organize collecting the poor contorted body.

We went the next morning and got Fan and
buried her and put stones over her grave. We
buried her just opposite the barn in the
woods near that post and little Max every few
minutes would run and sit on her grave and
cry. We do miss her very much.

Willie's handwriting looped wildly. He had been as upset as Max, but he didn't show it in the same way. Poor Max believed that Fanny had died because he had committed some wicked sin. "I will be good," his little brother wailed. Bella and Jennie had cried just as much. Willie could not permit himself many tears. He tried to comfort Bella, Jennie, and Max with scriptures and prayers. A real minister would have known what to say, but Willie could only do his best. Surely God would comfort them and punish the perpetrator of the dastardly deed.

Willie resumed writing, holding his pen in firm control.

> But that can't be helped. If you should see another little dog like her to bring it along with you... but I guess you would find it a hard job to get another faithful little dog as faithful as she was...
>
> It is now nearly noon and time to go home for my dinner. I am carrying out business as well as can be done. I am keeping track of my hours, and will be able to give you a receipt for my services when you get home. I must close now giving my best love to you from me and all the others.
> > I remain your loving son
> > William Lyon Mackenzie King

Later that afternoon, Willie was in the garden, scuffling a long row of potatoes. "Sciff scritch," went the hoe. A lone crow cawed from the big pine tree.

Where are Bella and Jennie? Willie wondered. *I could use a drink.*

They'll be coming soon with the bucket of cool ice water, he thought. He decided to stop work and wait for them in the shade. He lay back in the tickly grass and watched the branches wave above, slowly fanning the lazy midsummer sky.

I miss Fanny, Willie realized. Normally, her panting black body would be lying beside him, her pink tongue lolling out of her mouth, her tail thumping happily every time her young master spoke or patted her shaggy head. "I miss Fan," he half-whispered aloud.

Again the crow cawed. A grey squirrel scampered up a nearby maple. Willie looked once more into the pattern of the branches and the sky. Mesmerized, his mind slipped into wondering and dreaming.

What purpose does the Creator have for me? I am sure it is to do good, to be as good a man as my father, to be as great a man as my grandfather. I feel I am meant to help others less fortunate than me, but I do not yet know how. Father, in his talks, has begun to prepare me for university. Mother too, is encouraging me. What, what shall I be?

"Do you know?" he asked out loud to the saucy squirrel, which had curiously come near him. The squirrel churred, flicked its tail in alarm, and scurried back to its tree. Willie laughed.

"I didn't think you knew any better than I," he said and returned to his silent reverie. Would he be a lawyer like Papa? His father had recently been appointed a Queen's Counsel. Law seemed a noble profession. Or a minister? That way he would help people and please God. Or would he enter a life of public service? He often thought he would be a politician like Grandfather and maybe, maybe even one day return to Woodside, beloved Woodside, and purchase it. The reward after a life of helping others. *Perhaps, perhaps...* and his dreams became fuzzy, golden and warm.

On his way. Willie graduates with a master's degree from the
University of Toronto (1897) and one from Harvard (1898).

2

Deeds Worthy of Showing

University of Toronto
Toronto, Ontario
October, 1891

"Let's go on an expedition, lads!" King proposed. "Let's hike out over to the cemetery and visit the grave of Toronto's first mayor and hero of the people."

"Your grandfather, you mean?" asked his longtime friend from Berlin, Louis Breithaupt.

"Of course!" King smiled.

"It's a grand day," his college pal Bert Harper pointed out. "Let's go!" Harper and Breithaupt were as eager as King to explore their new surroundings.

Looking smart in their new suits and hats, the three young men set out. The city near the University of Toronto boomed with the sounds of industrial growth. As they made their way through streets filled with bustling carts and trolley cars, the students couldn't help notice that not all of Toronto's 181,000 souls were in step with the march toward progress. Many recently arrived immigrants were homeless. The boys passed alleys where entire families camped out despite the chill of the autumn nights. When King saw the faces of dirty and hungry children he wondered how things got that way and what he could do to make them better.

When the young men entered the cemetery, the angry din of the city was replaced with a golden-green peace. The autumn sun smiled, the leaves danced down from the trees and fell onto the quiet memorials of the generations who, King believed, had gone on to greater glory.

Although he couldn't remember quite where the grave was, as if led by instinct, Willie led the little band in search of Mackenzie's burial site. "Here it is!" he called out before long.

When the boys gathered around Mackenzie's grave, King almost couldn't speak. It was such a powerful moment, reverently observing the hallowed spot and seeing friends' faces, quietly impressed.

King held his hat in his hands and briefly closed his eyes. He thought of all his grandfather had worked to accomplish in his life. But the poor suffered as much as they had in the days when the elder William Lyon was alive. His grandson should change things. Surely he would accomplish some great work before he died!

Silently, King renewed his vow to become as great a man as he could and to help others. At university he would prepare himself for his life's work, whatever God showed him it would be.

∽

A few days later he wrote about his experiences in a letter home. Often, Willie missed his family. He decorated his stark room at the boarding house with their pictures. The largest one centred over the mantelpiece was a photograph of his father looking noble in his legal robes. Willie was proud that his father, a former student of the university and now serving on its senate, was highly regarded by young and old alike. In fact, Willie introduced himself to some of his classmates as the son of "Senator Rex" of Berlin. The nickname stuck, and Willie became known as Rex to his closest friends.

Like any eighteen-year-old living in a big city and away from his parents for the first time, Rex had a lot of fun sampling the social aspects of university life. He was always in a laughing group of students, at dances, the theatre, sports matches, and Glee Club events. Willie enjoyed the company of his friends and especially his female acquaintances. In King's circle it seemed there was always a beautiful young lady whom he admired. For a while, the lovely Mab Moss received his attentions, but he never let himself become distracted for too long.

To enter into his life's mission King wanted to have his body, mind, and soul at their best. To keep his body in shape he worked out at the gym and continued to play sports such as cricket and football. To strengthen his soul he prayed every day, attended church, and devoted his spare time to good works, such as visiting sick children in the hospital. To sharpen his mind he joined the debating club, spoke at political clubs, and studied, studied, studied.

King had entered a relatively new area of study at the University of Toronto – political science. He worked hard to get good marks – even put notes on his bedpost so he could revise while dressing! In 1893 he was quite pleased when his hard work paid off when he was awarded the Blake Scholarship. He was also proud when he was voted president of his class. His family wrote to congratulate him. Bella teased: "You seem such a young boy to make President but I hope in every way the position you have attained will bring much pleasure to all about you & that you will act in a way becoming the grandson of the late William Lyon Mackenzie. Is not that a speech?"

Being smart and having friends wasn't enough for King. He was always pushing himself to do more. In 1893 he began to write about his struggle for betterment in his private diary, a journal that he would keep until a few days before he died. In his diary he would chart his dreams, detail his daily activities, bemoan his shortcomings, and crow his victories. On September 6, 1893 he earnestly penned the first entry:

> This diary is to contain a very brief sketch of the events, actions, feelings and thoughts of my daily life. It must above all be a true and

faithful account. The chief object of my keeping this diary is that I may be ashamed to let even one day have nothing worthy of its showing, and it is hoped that through its pages the reader may be able to trace how the author sought to improve his time.

In his ascension to goodness and greatness, Willie drew inspiration from those around him. He brushed elbows with the noted intellectual Goldwin Smith. When the Kings left Woodside they moved to Toronto, and rented a house from the Smiths. John King, now a lecturer at Osgoode Hall, was a friend of the famous man. Smith's thoughts on economics and the unfulfilled potential of Canada as an independent nation fuelled many spirited conversations. Now the family was happily gathered together again – in the library of the house on Grange Road – to discuss matters of the changing world.

Willie also talked to his family about the biographies of the famous reformers he had read. He was particularly inspired when he read Arnold Toynbee. Toynbee was a British economist and humanitarian who had worked himself to death in 1883 at age thirty-one from his efforts to help the poor. King read how Toynbee Hall had been opened in an immigrant section of London as a haven for the poor and a centre of education. There the well-off and educated could live and work with their less fortunate brothers and sisters. After reading Toynbee's essays on the working class in the Industrial Revolution, King "was simply enraptured by his writings…" He confessed to his diary "I have at last found a model for my future work in life." He also attended talks at a conference on Education and Religion given by another person who had been inspired by Toynbee. The famous American settlement worker, Miss Jane Addams, had been spurred to action by Toynbee's example. Willie was thinking that social work combined with the ministry might be a fine way to make a difference in the world.

Willie was aware that politicians were also people who had the power to perform good works. He greatly admired the famous Liberal Prime Minister William Ewart Gladstone, who had just served his fourth term as prime minister of Britain. The young student knew that one of the earliest good works the politician had performed was to rescue girls who had "fallen" into prostitution.

Above all these examples of thinking and acting people was Grandfather. With his eyes opened wide, Willie read a biography of Mackenzie written by Uncle Charles Lindsey. He was especially stirred by Mackenzie's love of the poor, "the humble and the lowly." He felt his grandfather's blood "coursing through my veins," and his heart beat more quickly with resolve to make his mark by helping others.

∽

Sick Children's Hospital, Toronto
January 6, 1894
King watched the little girl on the bed struggle with death. Her breathing was so shallow that it could not be heard over the gentle swish, swish of the nurses' long starched skirts as they came and went.

"Katie," he said softly. Her eyes fluttered open. "Shall I say a prayer? Shall we pray that your family will draw nearer our Lord as you have?" he asked her. "Then they will have a beautiful home in the hereafter," he continued, "just like the one that waits for you."

Katie smiled, but she could no longer speak. King began to pray out loud. In his mind, he also prayed that soon Katie's earthly suffering would end and her eternal reward begin.

Almost every Sunday since he had arrived in Toronto, King had conducted religious services and read *Sunbeam* stories to the children at the Sick Children's Hospital. He loved his time with the eager children and the dear nurses, whom he also sought to guide towards eternal life through letters and talks.

When Katie Cameron's bright little spark went out, King thought about what she had told him about the terrible life she had lived. She had confidentially confessed some of the things that she and her sister had done to survive. King knew it was time to do more, to take his work beyond the hospital walls. Shortly after the last hymns were sung at little Katie's funeral, Willie called on her parents. Next he went to see her sister and spoke to her about stopping "her wicked life" and turning to Christ. Nina cried a little and seemed ready to repent. Encouraged, King went back to visit her another time at Mrs. Sherman's boarding house, but instead learned she was at a different house on King Street. When he arrived he found "a young fellow there, a perfect scoundrel, I believe, who has wished to marry her, but she refused him and decided to come with me to Mrs. Sherman's." Once there they had a long, quiet talk, "a little hymn and a little prayer."

Over the next while King devoted a lot of energy to helping Nina. In his diary, he never really says what she was doing, but despite her good intentions, it seems change wasn't possible. A few months later Nina was arrested and imprisoned for theft. Shortly after, young King, like his hero Gladstone, tried to help a prostitute, but his efforts weren't as persistent after he had met failure with Nina.

His time prior to graduation was very busy, filled with social work and political activities. King had become involved with a student strike to protest favouritism in hiring staff and the wrongful dismissal of a professor at the university. Before a large crowd of his classmates, Rex spoke excitedly against the "tyranny" of the university administration and called for a government investigation. The university did not seem to appreciate his actions. Shortly after his graduation with a Bachelor of Arts degree in 1895, King applied for a scholarship so he could do a master's degree at the University of Toronto. His request was denied. Willie and his parents were furious.

Willie had made the same application to the University of Chicago and was cheerfully offered a small scholarship. At that time, King felt it was impossible to continue his education. His family was swimming in debt and Max was eying university too. Finances were so bad that John took out another loan and Bella and Jennie were thinking of taking up jobs to help! Willie decided to work for a year and study independently. In the evenings he and a friend studied for their law degrees under John King's watchful eye. Willie earned money by tutoring others, and he also found employment in a series of writing jobs with Toronto papers.

He knew he didn't want to be a journalist and he was coming to the conclusion that he didn't want to be a practising lawyer either. His father was disappointed, but Willie continued to study so that he could at least have a degree in law. He wasn't sure which career he should chose – minister, politician, social worker or – who knew – professor? Clearly he needed more education. King soothed himself with the thought that his work on his master's degree was merely postponed. He wrote in his diary that covering police court and other stories was a good way to see "the shadowy side of life, looking at everything from an eco[nomic] standpoint. I will derive great benefit from my after work. I fully intend to made academic work my profession and am taking journalism as an entire year of practical example in the great school of life."

By spring his life would change.

∞

Toronto
May 2, 1896
King spent the morning in court covering the story of two fourteen-year-old girls who had been arrested for the theft of several rings. It had been the usual morning of the sublime and the ridiculous, with fainting and other dramatic effects, to which, by now, he was accustomed. After the girls had been sentenced to jail, and

court had adjourned, King left the dreary courthouse and went out into the lovely spring sunshine. He had a shave and a shoeshine and then did some shopping. He bought a silk tie and some kid gloves for evening outings and a cane of Congo oak with a silver tip. He left the walking stick at Kent's to have his initials, *W.L.M.K.*, engraved on it for an extra fifteen cents.

With a jaunty step, he strolled on to meet his friend Henry Kingstone. The two set off to keep a theatre date with Charlie Cross, Willie's partner in his legal studies. On the way there they called on an old lady by the name of Mrs. Menden. Mrs. Menden was a fortuneteller. She divulged some "strange truths" to Willie.

> She said I had left study for a while and was at commercial work (newspaper) which was a pity. I should keep at the other profession.
>
> Had thought of ministry and might get into it. Tho' now not as religious as I ought to be.
>
> That my initials were W. M. and last name King, first name Willie.
>
> I was fond of intellectual girls, and did not care particularly for dances etc.
>
> Was fond of children, and practical.
>
> Would live to be old and would be successful.
>
> Wd. go to Chicago this fall and wd. hear of appointment in about 10 days.

Four days later King had a letter from the University of Chicago once again offering him a fellowship to study political economics and sociology. King Senior was pleased. So was Isabel, although she cried and slept badly. Willie would be leaving them.

Willie knew he could not miss this opportunity to begin fulfilling his dreams. In Chicago he hoped to study, do original work, and take steps towards achieving his goals. He told himself that he would be nearer the masses he wanted to serve more seriously, so that he would be "drawn closer to the living God." Willie had no rest, for there was a voice that whispered, night and day, *Go to Chicago, go to Chicago*. He packed his trunk.

∞

Hull-House, Nineteenth Ward
Chicago, Illinois, United States
January 7, 1897
"I am afraid, Miss Addams," King said, nervously tapping his fingers on the desk in front of him, "that money is not my sole consideration."

Not long after he arrived in Chicago in the early autumn of 1896, King had called on Jane Addams at Hull-House. Addams had helped found this inner-city settlement house in one of the city's "worst" districts in 1889. Here, as at the Toynbee Hall settlement house in England, people came to teach and live with the poor. Addams and her volunteer workers hoped they were giving their charges the tools they needed to address the wrongs in their horrible living and working conditions. Volunteers helped men, women, and children, many of them immigrants, learn to read and write. They established kindergartens and worked to change legislation. They held enthusiastic talks on literature, art, health, childcare, worker safety, and industrial unions. In October, at Addams's invitation, King had eagerly taken up residence at Hull-House. Now, only a few months later, he was informing Addams that he could not go on as a volunteer. Thinking the issue was money, Addams responded by looking at the young student with understanding brown eyes and offering him a small salary.

"I enjoy the speeches and my work," King yammered uncomfortably, "but it is walking and taking the train from Hull-House, for two hours each day through misery, wretchedness, vice and degradation, abomination, filthiness and noise to classes where I must concentrate! It is just too much!" Willie babbled. "In fact, I consulted my doctor as I'm afraid I'm about to have a nervous breakdown. Furthermore," he added sincerely, "I do not feel I'm doing either job well. I think I will better be able to help others if I complete my master's degree first."

"Of course," Addams agreed, sympathetically. Suddenly they heard a crash followed by a wail from one of the kindergarten rooms. Addams was on her feet and off to divert a catastrophe. The interview was over. With over two thousand souls to care for each week Addams was very busy. Perhaps, after all, she didn't have time to understand.

King felt rebuffed for but a moment. He reminded himself his work lay in his studies. He would work hard and he *would* do good.

∞

Toronto
September 19, 1897
William Mulock, the postmaster general, had the appearance of a staid Victorian gentleman. With his white beard and formal poise, he looked like someone who might have dismissed the young man before him as a wet-behind-the-ears whipper-snapper.

Young King had come to Mulock to divulge terrible wrongs that he had discovered were going on right under the government's eyes – even with the government's sanction, he had almost suggested. "My mind was ablaze!" King passionately confessed as he described the investigation he had done for an article on the terrible conditions of the garment trade. "Women work long hours for a few pennies!" King contended. "And the work they were doing in these sweat shops was sewing letter carrier uniforms." Government contracts, King had discovered, had been subcontracted to men who unfairly ran "sweat shops" and drew huge profits while the workers were paid pittances.

For a number of reasons Mulock heard out the clean-shaven, energetic young man with courtesy and patience. Mulock and John King were colleagues and friends, whose families moved in the same social circles. John had suggested his son speak to Mulock before he sent results of his investigation to print. When he was vice-chancellor at the University of Toronto, Mulock had seen young King and learned something of his interest in labour, politics, and philosophy. Mulock was now postmaster general and a Liberal member in the House of Commons. As the century drew to a close, he was one of Prime Minister Laurier's party men listening to changing ideas and aware that the Liberals would need young people with new skills and energies to carry them out. He was interested in seeing how bright young King's fire might burn.

"What do you suggest?" he asked calmly.

"A study!" Willie answered without hesitation. "The government could hire me to carry out a study of the matter with suggestions for reforming the system."

"That," Mulock replied slowly, "is a good idea."

Willie worked on the landmark study and completed his master's thesis on the International Typographical Union during 1897. One other very important event in his life occurred that year. During the winter he spent three weeks at St. Luke's Hospital recovering from typhoid fever. His stay was just long enough that he became enamoured with nurse Mathilde Grosset, a woman with lovely wavy hair, an intriguing German accent, and a "beautiful Christian character." By spring of 1898 King's fancy had turned to thoughts of love, to the point where he was preparing to marry his nurse. He pictured himself assuming his grandfather's mantle, fighting for right with his beloved by his side.

His family brought him back to earth with a crash. Father, Mother, and sister Jennie provided a united front – a forceful wave of sternly reproaching letters.

They reminded Willie that he had not finished his education or even begun a career, which was unfair to the girl and to himself. Furthermore, *they* counted on him, Father pointed out, as his "first duty is to those at home." Even Jennie royally chastised him, but Mother wrote the most scathing letter. She complained how she was growing weary with age. She solicited his charity not so much for herself, but for his sisters. "I have built castles without number for you," she reminded him. "Are all these dreams but to end in dreams?"

Although King agonized, in a few months it was clear the affair would end. He spent the summer healing his wounds and expanding his prospects. "A man's success very much depends on his social qualities," his father had taught him. King summered with the wealthy Gerry family, tutoring their two sons. In summers previous to this he had visited Bert near Barrie, Ontario and paddled schoolgirls about on the Muskoka lakes. Now he stayed in the United States, on Rhode Island, tasted his first sip of champagne, and was within smiling distance of the cultured Miss Julia Grant, granddaughter of American Civil War hero and president, Ulysses S. Grant. King still had no position and wasn't sure whether he would have a career in the hallowed halls of academia or elsewhere. But he was twenty-five, had education and connections, and his future, ah, his future was bright.

He received a master's degree from the University of Toronto in 1897 and another from Harvard in 1898. He began studies in political science and work at Harvard on a PhD. He would later complete his PhD dissertation on "Oriental Immigration to Canada," but when Harvard granted him a travelling scholarship, he eagerly set off to discover Europe. While he took in the breathtaking scenery of Britain, France, Switzerland, and Italy, he got to know important people who might be of help one day.

One day in late June after he had been cycling with a friend in the countryside around Rome, Rex was heading to his hotel room when the desk clerk called out "Signor King, a telegram." With amazement he read:

June 26, 1900
Will you accept the editorship and management of new Government *Labor Gazette*, Ottawa? Begin duties early in July. Salary fifteen hundred dollars. May increase. If yes, come. Wm. Mulock

Mulock had not forgotten him, and his proposition was intriguing. The Dominion government was just beginning to form a department for Labour. King could be in on the ground floor.

However, Harvard was also offering him a position as lecturer in political economics. What to do, what to do? A position with the civil service with the government of Canada or one in the halls of Harvard?

I still have work to do, King thought, remembering his unfinished doctorate. He decided to decline Canada's offer.

3

The Dream of My Life

Gatineau Hills, Quebec
Thanksgiving Day, 1900
"Season of mists and mellow fruitfulness! Close bosom-friend of the maturing sun…" Bert Harper surveyed the autumn scene and quoted a few lines from Keats's poem "To Autumn." Just outside Ottawa, King Mountain was glorious in its autumn colours – fiery reds and oranges leaped into the blue sky. Below, the waters of King Lake winked merrily in the sunshine.

"Any regrets, old man?" Harper asked.

"Sometimes whoever seeks abroad may find," King continued the poem. "Regrets? On a day like this, seated in the bountiful lap of nature? But for the fact

William Lyon Mackenzie King, M.P. (North Waterloo, Ontario)
and Minister of Labour, December 1910. A Windsor suit still
hangs smartly at Laurier House, Ottawa, Ontario.

you are eating all the chicken! The cycling up here has made you as greedy as a lion."

Harper laughed, but this didn't stop him from helping himself to another piece of chicken from the plate on the checkered picnic cloth. He lazily continued the conversation between mouthfuls. "You know what I mean, Rex. Europe, Harvard, all that! Any regrets about changing your mind and giving it up for a desk job in Ottawa?"

"A desk job in Ottawa?" King exclaimed. "I am King of the desks!" He leapt up on a boulder and took a mock strongman stance. "I am editor of the *Labor Gazette* – produced, I may add, with the worthy Mr. Henry Albert Harper, my friend, colleague, and roommate. I am deputy minister of labour, the youngest deputy minister in the history of Canada. I have seen the groundwork I laid built into the Fair Wages Resolution Act, striking down the use of sweat shop labour for government contracts. I am now truly carrying on the work of my grandfather, able to influence those who might do something for the working classes!"

"Hear, hear!" Harper encouraged, his brown eyes bright with glee.

"Why," King said pridefully, "if my spirit and my resolve stay strong, I may even enter public life. I am but twenty-six. One day," he paused, looking at the grand vista before him, "should it be the will of the God of Bethel, I may be premier of this country."

Harper mumbled his approval through a mouthful of grapes.

King grabbed up a bunch of grapes and began strutting with his chest puffed out like a peacock, "We are young gods, you and I. By day I earn an income larger than many at Harvard, enough to provide for my needs and amply assist my family. By night, I am wined and dined in the best homes in the company of some of the fairest young maidens in our nation's capital. Regrets? None have I!"

Harper chuckled at his friend's performance. Rex unpuffed himself and questioned, "How about you, Harper? Any regrets?"

"None. The work I am helping you do is important – much different from covering Ottawa stories for the *Montreal Gazette*. Still, there are one or two *jeunes filles* in the office I miss!" he lamented.

"Good heavens man, how many girls can you handle? Last night you were out with Miss Campbell, tomorrow we're lunching with the Sherwood sisters, and I know you've been corresponding with my sister Jennie!"

Harper smiled, and rolled over to survey the wonders of the sky – so blue, so crisp, so perfect, with only one or two slightly grey clouds chuffing into view – nothing to ruin their day.

"We're fortunate Reverend Herridge recommended this place," he sighed happily.

"Yes. You know, Bert," King mused, "I wouldn't mind having a little place out here. Wouldn't it be lovely, summering with the Herridges and having Mother and Father come for holidays?"

"Is it a holiday with your mother or father you're dreaming of, or one nearer the lovely Mrs. Herridge?"

King pelted a grape at him.

King and Harper worked in the new Department of Labour under the auspices of the postmaster general. The federal government was just beginning to transform itself into a buzzing beehive of expanded services, and the young civil servants were part of a growing swarm of workers. As editor of the *Labor Gazette* King was so busy that his brother Max joked that he only got up from his desk to visit the backhouse.

Postmaster General Mulock had hired the young man for more than his editorial skills. As Canada adjusted itself to the thought of trade unions, the government needed someone knowledgeable in the field of labour to address a growing number of strikes. As the affable deputy minister returned from more and more missions of strike investigation, the postmaster general came to appreciate the young man's gift of conciliation. Letters praising his tact came into the office from city officials, union representatives, *and* factory owners. King began serving on Royal Commissions looking into labour disputes from Quebec to British Columbia.

∞

Union Station, Toronto
December, 1901
"Cold!" King couldn't help remarking to the conductor when the train door opened and an icy blast of air hit him. "It's still tropical in B.C. even though it's December," he rued. He stepped off the train with a confident air, despite the fact that his business at Rossland had been unsuccessful. He'd stop in Toronto to visit his family for a few days. Then he would go

back to Ottawa to give a full report about how the stubborn employers and aggressive union leaders had blocked progress in resolving the miners' strike. Usually King was more successful.

He passed a newspaper boy shouting the latest headline: "Ottawa in shock! Two skaters die while many look on!" King handed the lad a coin and took one of the papers.

He scanned the story.

Two drown in Ottawa River, as hero selflessly attempts to save girl. Bessie Blair of Ottawa was a member of a skating party that had ventured too near thin ice. The ice cracked beneath her, and the freezing waters swirled around her. While other skaters looked on, one young man, thoughtless of the risk to himself, rushed to her aid. Jumping in after her he cried, "What else can I do?" Those were the last words of Henry Albert Harper of Ottawa.

Henry Albert Harper of Ottawa, King read again. The fist of terror beat his brain, and another pummelled him in the stomach. "Bert!" he gasped aloud.

∞

Despite the support of his family, it seemed impossible to get over the death of Bert. When he returned to Ottawa, the minister's friendly wife, Mrs. Herridge, was one of the first to provide solace. Many people of

Ottawa shared King's shock at the tragedy. The city erected a bronze statue of Sir Galahad near the Parliament Buildings in memory of Harper. King wrote a book about his friend and called it *The Secret of Heroism*. But nothing seemed to take away the pain, and nothing filled the void of the horrible loss. King thought he might never enjoy such a deep friendship again.

Bert had given everything to try and save the life of one person. King would dedicate his life to trying to improve the lives of many, to achieve the noble goal set by his grandfather and pursued by his dear friend, both now gone. He threw himself in to his duties.

He carried on the work that he and Harper had begun with the *Labor Gazette* in addition to his duties of deputy minister. Again and again he criss-crossed the county, seeking settlement to strikes through investigation. Accumulating information enabled King to get both sides talking. Then he emphasized the points the different parties had in common. "Investigation is letting in the light," King felt. Prime Minister Laurier noted the work of this rising civil servant and had occasion to test King's skills.

A strike in the Alberta coal mines begun in March 1906 still continued in the winter of 1907. People were burning twisted straw or anything they could get their hands on to keep from freezing. "Do you think you can do something?" Prime Minister Laurier asked the young civil servant. "Yes I can," King answered firmly. After an inquiry, he discovered that the issues of union recognition, wage increases, and reduced hours had been overlooked. King managed to smooth things out.

Of more importance to the country was the fact these experiences provided insights that helped him to draft the Industrial Disputes Investigation Act. King cobbled bits of information together about acts in other countries and brought in some of the things he had used to draft the Railway Labour Disputes Act. The Industrial Disputes Act of 1907 called for postponement of a strike or lockout in mines or public utilities until an investigation at public expense could be arranged. King was sure the period of delay provided by the investigation would also help irate tempers cool off. Canada was one of the first countries to enact this sort of legislation.

Prime Minister Laurier was aware that the act had been created largely by a civil servant – one who was attracting more and more attention. King had done well on the national scene, but how was he at playing ball on an international court?

As deputy minister of labour, King had been involved with immigration issues. Many Canadian labourers were concerned about the increasing number of immigrants from India, Japan, and China who would work for next to nothing and even as strike-breakers. On the West Coast, the situation turned ugly in 1907 when rioters expressed their outrage in violence. As part of a Royal Committee, King explored the problems that had led up to the riot and the resulting property losses to the Japanese and Chinese communities of Vancouver. At the invitation of President Theodore Roosevelt, he also went to the United States to hear American concerns.

Laurier sent King to Britain to meet with officials from the India and Colonial Offices. Amazingly, King was able to find a diplomatic solution to the problem. He pointed out that legislation that already existed in the Indian Emigration Act forbade Indians to emigrate under contract to work in Canada. Laurier was pleased with King's performance.

The Governor General, Earl Grey, saw that King was awarded the Companion of the Order of St. Michael and St. George, a very high honour for a civil servant. Now Willie felt he was ready to leave the civil service and set his sights a little higher.

∞

Berlin, Ontario
September 24, 1908
King roared into town like a general to the front. There was an election to fight, and he had let Laurier know he was determined to win. He drove his assistants to mount the attack. He drilled businessmen on the issues, organized them into squadrons, and sent them door to door. He personally greeted platoons of people, impressed many by greeting them by name, and won them over with his charm and good humour. He worked tirelessly, editing copy until 2 a.m., his pencil going slash, slash, slash, until his speeches became the sharp weapons with which he would courteously, but meticulously, cut down his opponents.

Today, other Liberal politicians of note were on the scene to help him with his fight. The bunting fluttered in the breeze as the Right Honourable Sir Wilfrid Laurier took to the stage. A throng of thousands had gathered, and all were enthralled with his Old World gallantry and grace. As Laurier turned to his young protégé, his face lit with a smile. King wore an immaculate dark suit, a starched collar, a tie pin placed in his tie in the fashion that Laurier wore his. The aspiring politician looked into the eyes of the great Liberal leader, noted the spirit and fire, but worried that he also detected a weary and feeble note in Laurier's demeanour.

Laurier turned to the eagerly listening crowd. "I am of the belief that the Department of Labour needs to be its own department with its own minister. Furthermore, I am delighted with this young man," he enthused. "He is definitely cabinet material. It is simply up to the people of North Waterloo to elect him!"

When the applause died, King took his place before the podium. Another ovation. He looked at the sea of expectant faces before him and experienced the rush of excitement he felt every time he stepped before a crowd. "My friends of North Waterloo!" he began.

By spring of 1909 the newspapers were writing about the new minister of labour, the "Honourable Mackenzie King, one of the best-groomed men in Cabinet, Solver of Labour Troubles."

∞

Kingsmere, Quebec
August, 1910
"Father's complaining about the insects. I think he's using it as an excuse to lie down for a rest," Bella giggled, "but I'm ready to go out in the canoe!"

It made Willie happy to have Father, Mother, and Bella at Kingsmere on holiday. Max, now a doctor, practised medicine near by in Ottawa. Jennie had her own family in Wiarton and would undoubtedly come for holidays too.

Willie realized that his father had never built a cottage or even owned property. Finally he was able to make up to him and his dear little mother for some of the sacrifices they had made.

"I'll just check to see if Mother doesn't want to come too. I'll be along in a moment."

Even though it was a warm day, a small fire was lit in the grate. Isabel sat next to it, a book open on her lap. *How beautiful she looks*, King thought. *The purest soul God ever made.* The firelight made her cheeks rosy, and her white curls fluffed like soft feathers around her face. She was in the exact pose of one of the paintings King had commissioned of her.

"Now Mother, is that book Morley's *The Life of Gladstone: The Prime Minister*, the one you have in your portrait?" her son teased. "If that's the one you're reading I'll think you're posing for your painting again."

"But you will be a regular Gladstone!" Isabel laughed, a frequent and pleasant sound. "Aren't we in high spirits today, Billy?"

"Why not! My family is with me and it's a lovely day. Hardly any need for a fire."

"You know how easily I feel a chill these days. Besides it is such a lovely fireplace with a fire in it."

"It's a copy of the one Shakespeare had at Stratford-on-Avon and I've dedicated it to Bert," he said quietly. "Although I'm not so sure dear Bert's spirit hasn't become quite mischievous. It smokes a lot at times! Now Mother, are you coming out on the lake?"

"You go ahead, but be careful," she warned. "Sir Wilfrid doesn't want to lose his minister of labour. Oh Willie, Father and I were so proud. We were looking down from the galleries as Sir Wilfrid introduced you to the house. "William Lyon Mackenzie King. The name rang out across the room."

"I was proud of *you* Mother. The press had so many things to say about you – how distinguished and witty you are, how much you look like Grandfather. I was so happy to see you and Father there. If only Grandfather could have been present to see me carrying on his work, my happiness would have been complete."

Willie put a poker in the fire and stirred the flame brighter.

"It's all been so wonderful, Mother, the dream of my life. It's as if an unseen hand guides me in the direction of my life's work. One step after the other I have been led up to this height. College, settlement life, post-graduate study, the Bill, the recognition from the Crown, my doctorate from Harvard for my work on Oriental Immigration, all come as if Fate or Destiny was guiding me in the direction of a living. Now, with the election, the voice of the people is calling me to come as their champion in the fight for a greater liberty." King thrust the poker back into the stand and turned to look directly at her, his cheeks flushed. "Surely my success can erase the blot of the rebellion, if ever a blot it was!"

"I cannot but feel that you are going on with a work that your grandfather strove hard to throw the best part of his life into, and now you will too. But Willie," she continued in a confidential tone, "you are thirty-five years of age. Don't you think that it might be time to settle down?"

"Are you plotting with Sir Wilfrid and Lady Zoë?" Willie asked her, chuckling. "They've been asking me to dine with them and a number of young ladies, all of them wealthy. I think of them as skirmishing expeditions. Laurier thinks that such a wife is what I'll need to secure a foothold with my public career."

"Sir Wilfrid is a wise man!" Isabel enthused.

"Mother," he said, taking up one of her hands, "what Sir Wilfrid does not know is that until I find a young lady who is even *half* as good as you, I will not be content. I will not let wealth, position, or aught else tempt me."

"Willleeeee!" a screech was heard from towards the docks.

"That lovely voice would be Bella. Come for a paddle, Mother," Willie urged, "for I won't hear anything different."

<hr>

"Tell me more of what happened," King gently urged the woman.

"The phosphorous from the matches in the factory where she worked. The doctor says phosphorous poisoning made my daughter die. It was horrible to watch her swell up and suffer, all because she wanted to help feed us." The woman bowed her head.

"When did she begin work in the factory?"

"She started at age fourteen and she was there for seven years. When she died she was only just turned twenty," the grieving mother whispered.

"Mrs. LeBlanc, what wages did Thérèse earn?"

"They paid her $1.25 per day."

"Tell me about her illness." King felt himself shuddering inwardly. He hoped it wasn't as bad as some of the stories he'd been told about disintegrating jawbones from the long-term contact with phosphorous. One woman had choked to death from the puss of her abscesses. Another he had talked to had no lower jaw and told King that she'd pulled out her own jawbone – that's how bad the infection had been.

"Well, first she had a toothache and then her jaws began to ache and finally her whole face was swelled up like!" The woman showed with her hands how big the swelling had been. "She went to the hospitals for two operations, but it did no good. In the end she was blind. And then, she d... d... d... " the woman faltered and could no longer speak.

King wrote everything down. He knew that white phosphorous caused painful and horrible death through phosphorus necrosis. Permitting such industrial conditions was intolerable. His report and subsequent bill would make a difference.

∽

Office of the Minister
Department of Labour, Ottawa
September 22, 1911
King picked up the human jawbone of one of the victims and prepared to pack it into box along with the other items that had been on his desk.

"Hideous," he muttered.

The Act to Prohibit the Manufacture, Importation and Sale of Matches Made With White Phosphorous would not be passed in 1911. On September 21, 1911, the Laurier government had lost the election and so had King. These and other bills would have to remain dreams – for the time being.

"But they will happen," he promised.

King (with cane) and John D. Rockefeller, Jr., 1915.

4

Duty, Death

Colorado, United States
April 3, 1915

"No, no, don't get up." Willie protested. His brother Max sank down on the sofa. "You're looking much better," Willie noted. Max had moved to Colorado in an attempt to recover from tuberculosis – a dreaded and often fatal disease. "How's the book coming?" King cheerfully asked the ill man.

"Wonderfully well," Max replied. "I'm so glad, Billy, that you encouraged me. There is so much people can learn about how to beat TB."

Max's wife, May, came into the room, two boys, twins, toddling beside her. "Go see your uncle, Arthur," she encouraged. "Lyon, it's your Uncle Willie, the one you're named after!"

King, on his knees, hugged his nephews.

He spent some time with the family, catching them up to date on how his work was going. One of the reasons he was in Colorado was related to some of the investigations of conditions in mines he was doing for his new employer, the Rockefeller Foundation. A huge benefit to this trip was that he could visit his dear brother.

King looked at Max, who with his curly hair and light blue eyes had inherited so much of Grandfather's looks. He also seemed to have a lot of his fighting Scottish spirit. Yet, with a flush in his cheeks his little brother appeared so fragile.

They exchanged some stories about the times they had spent together in Ottawa. Then King lovingly embraced his brother, before returning to his hotel.

∞

The next morning, King awoke to the sound of the telegraph boy knocking on the door. The message he delivered spun King into action. Bella was ill. They were summoning him home. King had checked the train timetables, contacted Max, and begun to pack by the time the second telegraph arrived. This telegraph caused him to sit down and cry. It was too late. Bella was dead.

"If only she had listened!" he told Max. "Her heart would not have worn out."

"I tried to get her to rest more," Max rued, "to give up the nonsense of working as a clerk at the bank.

With Mother and Father to look after, and her heart as weak as it is – was…" Max corrected himself, "it was all just too much. Our poor, dear gracious sister."

"She was such a good Christian, so loving to everyone. To Mother, to Father, to us, to the children she helped through St. Andrew's Church. I simply can't believe it," Willie shook his head, "Why now? Just when I was beginning to earn enough to be able to help lift her burden substantially."

King bade farewell to his brother and rushed to catch the train, thoughts flooding his brain. Dark and senseless the waves came, too fast and powerful to be stopped. *My sister. My big sister. Dead. No children, no spouse. I have just said goodbye to my brother. My little brother. Ill as he is, he gathers strength in the loving arms of his wife and children. I am over forty. What sort of life will I find? What sort of end? Bella. Why did you have to be taken now?*

∞

Colorado, United States
September, 1915
There was war in Europe, but the mood in the hall on this spring evening was one of optimism. The fiddlers were pushing the tempo. Someone yelped "Yahoo!" and the dancers on the floor stepped up their pace.

A handsome, compact man, with devilish dark eyes and a wicked smile, whirled his partner around, laughing gaily. The man was John D. Rockefeller, Junior, the richest person in the United States of America. The woman was the wife of one of his employees.

The year before, women and children had died violently in Ludlow, Colorado. The problems had begun in 1913 when the miners started protesting the conditions and the lack of union recognition at the coal mines in which Rockefeller was the largest shareholder. The workers left the company town and installed themselves and their families in tents, watched by the state militia and company guards. On the morning of April 20, 1914, men shooting rifles and machine guns attacked the tent village. They threw paraffin onto the tents and lit them on fire. Eleven children and two women had been burned to death and three camp leaders shot. The American nation had been shocked and had demanded action.

At the dance, the man who had succeeded in bringing change, William Lyon Mackenzie King, sat on the sidelines, sipping punch and chatting with the dancer's husband. Tonight he was enjoying one of his biggest successes.

At more than forty years of age and too old to fight in the war in Europe, King had had to find a job after the Liberals had lost the last election. He was looking after an increasing number of the bills for his parents and even for Max. His work at the *Canadian Liberal* and other small jobs didn't cover expenses. Nor did money from his friends. King had found a sympathetic patron, Violet Markham, an intelligent and wealthy British woman with a social conscience. He'd impressed Violet when he met her in 1905 and in the correspondence they'd established since. She was quite willing to help Rex financially while he was out of Parliament, in hope that he would soon return to power and advance the cause of the underprivileged. But King needed more money so that he could help his family. He felt it was necessary to take the well-paying job in the United States. As director of industrial investigations for the Rockefeller Foundation, he started at a $12,000 per year salary that in 1914 seemed sent from heaven. More importantly, King was not just carrying out an academic study of labour relations. He believed he could make a difference in the lives of many people.

He had several goals in mind when he took his New York job: one was remaining Canadian. He even conducted some business on letterhead that gave his Ottawa address. King did not want to jeopardize his aspirations for having a position with the Dominion government at some future date when the Liberals would return to power.

In his present post, King had to accept some of the restrictions of his employer. Despite public outcry, Rockefeller and his associates were not prepared to recognize the United Mine Workers of America. But Willie succeeded in having the Colorado Fuel and Iron Company recognize a union organized from within the company. Communication between the miners and their bosses was resumed, and the tension of the year before eased.

Rockefeller had re-established his reputation in the eyes of the public. He had even impressed Mother Jones, a well-known eighty-three-year-old labour activist. Moreover, he had impressed King as "one of the best men and most welcome of friends" and a fine Christian, someone who sincerely tried to help other men. *However*, King mused privately, as he watched his employer across the floor, *he's not the best dancer*.

"Not bad for a city slicker," the miner laughed, taking his wife's hand from Rockefeller.

"Mr. King taught me everything I know!" the industrialist joked. "Well, maybe not how to dance. But I certainly needed an education in labour and he gave it to me. I am but his mouthpiece."

The miner nodded his approval and led his wife onto the dance floor.

"You coming back with us to New York, old man?" Rockefeller asked between gulps of punch. "Or are you going to get some rest like the doctor ordered?"

Ignoring the comment about his state of fatigue from overwork, King replied, "Now that business is all but concluded, I think I'll see my brother."

"How is he?"

"Much better. The Colorado air has done him good. He's been able to move out of the sanatorium and is living nearby with his family in a small house."

"Sounds like he's on the road to recovery!" Rockefeller said.

King could not respond. When Max had first entered a sanatorium in Montreal, the doctor had confided to William that his brother would not recover from the deadly tuberculosis. He had not shared the news with Max. King told Rockefeller enthusiastically, "He's writing a book for other TB patients called *TB and How to Beat It!*"

"That's the spirit! You Kings – the harder you're hit, the higher you bounce."

King raised an eyebrow. That was exactly the phrase his brother had used when King had lost the 1911 election.

∞

Queen's Park, Toronto
September, 1916
King realized that he'd been walking around Queen's Park for some time – hours even. Now it was growing quite late. He sat down on a bench and tried to get hold of himself.

What day was it? What month? What year? 1916, the year. He couldn't figure out the exact day, but it must be one of the first days of September. His father had died August 30. His mother had left to stay with his sister Jennie that morning. It suddenly dawned on King that for the first time since he was a young man, he had no home in Toronto.

It seemed so impossible. Only a few short weeks before, his parents had been at Kingsmere. King remembered with regret, he had been sharp with his father. He didn't recall what it was over, but now he was filled with remorse. His father was but an old man. Though nearly blind he'd bravely gone off to teach classes until he had retired just last year. After Bella's death, John King had done his best to fumble through the streets doing the errands she had once done. His father did not deserve impatience, but that was how Willie had treated him the last time he saw him.

The last time he saw him. King moaned aloud.

How had it happened? Father had eaten something and apparently contracted food poisoning that quickly developed into unbearable pain. He'd died the next day.

It was unbelievable he was gone. Everyone was shocked. John King, the mentor of many – senator and professor at Osgoode, who had instructed over seven generations of law students; author and journalist admired by many editors; lawyer and expert in libel law, lauded by some of the best thinkers in the Dominion.

"And me?" King asked himself. He looked around but could see nothing save a blur before him. Father had steered him throughout his career – advised him to build his connections, to reach further and further. He had edited Willie's book about Bert and was helping him with his new manuscript. *He was always thinking of me, sacrificing for me and so proud. Such a good, moral person.* King began to cry, not caring whether people or pigeons saw his tears. *Dear, dear Father. I owe you more than I can express.* King looked at the darkening sky. *You, Father, gave me an example of the perfection of manhood. It is an example I will strive to follow.*

∞

Kingsmere, Quebec
August, 1917
"How much," King questioned the nurse, "can one person suffer?"

"Sh!" Nurse Petrie ordered. "She might hear you. Let her sleep now."

Willie bent near, kissed her forehead, and smoothed her beautiful white curls with a gentle hand. "Rest, Mother. The doctor will be here later."

King retreated to the next room and returned to the manuscript in his typewriter. Watching his mother suffer in his tiny rooms at the Roxborough apartment building through the winter of 1917 had nearly driven him mad. After her stroke, the doctor had diagnosed a condition he called atherosclerosis. The doctor had become a regular visitor, coming to drain away the putrid fluids that caused Mother to swell. Yet she seemed to get no better, so he had taken her to the country for a change of air.

What do the doctors know? Let Mother be at Kingsmere, nearer the flowers in the fields, the birds in the trees, the peace of nature she so enjoys. Why, I even carried her to the lake and had her christen the new wharf after Father and the new boathouse after herself, the Isabel Mackenzie King Boathouse. I will see to it that she will rally, gather her strength, and be fit for fall after a summer's idyll.

A search for personal peace was the second reason King had decamped from the city. When Rockefeller's business was not tapping at his shoulder, King was engaged in writing a book on labour relations. He needed quiet as he threw his soul into finishing *Industry and Humanity*. The pages had to contain all his thoughts on the relations between labourers, capital, management, and community. His experiences had led him to believe that government could have an increased role in helping to establish favourable relations between all parties. As the war drew to a close, the book preached a message of industrial peace and harmony that the world was so aching to hear. That was what King wanted – globally and at home: peace, harmony, and healing.

A few days later Isabel appeared much better.

"I knew the country air would set you right, Mother!" King crowed.

"Dear Willie, you always know what's best," Isabel demurred.

King squeezed his mother's hand. His heart swelled with love. "I only want the best for you, my dear. You are so brave."

He took the spoon from the nurse and finished feeding Isabel her applesauce.

"Mother, dare I speak again to you of my plans, my dream, my vision? You know that I have been called to be the voice of the Liberal party in North York – Grandfather's riding. I think they're soon to call an election... in the fall, but..." He looked into the dimming eyes, and was sure he saw a spark burning yet. He had to get back into Parliament. Public service was his life – but so was his mother.

"Billy..." She paused a moment, letting a little sigh of pain and weariness escape her lips. Then she smiled her reassurance and said, "I will be glad if you speak in your grandfather's voice."

∽

Roxborough Apartments, Ottawa
December 19, 1917
Grumpily, King paid the driver, arranged his baggage, and entered the Roxborough. He willed himself to

change his disgruntled look to one of joyful homecoming. The Laurier Liberals had lost the election. The Liberal Party had split on the conscription issue. King had stayed with Laurier, stayed with the Liberals and the anti-conscription stance that ensured their loss. Borden and the Conservatives had used the Wartime Elections Act to pump up the pro-conscription vote and entered the House to form a coalition government with the Union Liberals.

December 17, 1917 – Election Day. King would never forget it. What a way to spend his birthday!

The day after, he'd telephoned to let Mother, and Jennie, who was looking after her in Ottawa, hear the news from his own lips. He'd wished he had something more cheerful to tell them – Mother deserved to hear only good news.

Resolved to show his best face, he turned the door handle.

"Hello! Mother! I'm home!" he boomed.

Jennie came to the door. King immediately noticed the dark circles under her eyes.

He saw Nurse Petrie scuttling quickly away, carrying what appeared to be a box. Something was wrong.

King smelled the air. The heavy sickroom smell was still about – but it had changed. There was a melancholy note missing and a curiously, unidentifiably upsetting one in its place.

Something was very wrong. King charged towards his mother's bedroom, but Jennie stopped him.

"Mother?"

"She's… gone."

"When, Jennie, when?"

"The day after the election."
King crumpled with grief. *Bella, Father, Mother.*
One man can suffer immeasurably.

5

Nothing Will Be Impossible Unto You

Liberal Convention
Landsdowne Park, Ottawa
August 7, 1919

"I would like to borrow some poetic words of Tennyson to pay some slight tribute to the memory of our great and dearly beloved leader, Sir Wilfrid Laurier."

Excitement coursed through King like electricity. His face was shining like the sun. On the podium King was perfectly placed. In a large photograph on the wall behind him, Laurier, the recently deceased party leader, smiled with benevolent serenity. King's future was in the hands of the Liberal convention-goers

"This is a great favourite of mine," King wrote of this photo of himself taken during the Diamond Jubilee of Confederation celebration, July 1, 1927. "Hands and expression, position, uniform and all. Beautiful!"

before him. He was close to capturing the finest feather yet for his cap: leadership of a national party and the distinction of being the first leader to be elected at a national convention rather than selected by an elite group of peers.

King addressed the delegates as a strong man, only forty-four and eager to rebuild the party and bring the Liberal platform to the nation. He tried to convince the delegates that *he* could meld together the old and new to bring the party to triumph. Although a faithful Laurier Liberal, he was nonetheless prepared to welcome the Union Liberals back to the party and heal the deep schisms caused by wartime conscription. He would even extend the hand of friendship to members of the new parties – the Progressives and the United Farmers who could be persuaded to support the Liberal cause. His words of peace soothed the ears of the postwar audience.

King promised to seek harmony across the Dominion by finding commonality in the tariff, freight rates, and other problems now separating the agricultural west and industrial east. And who better than King the Conciliator to invite labour, community, and industry to the table to frame the future? Problems that had surfaced in the Winnipeg General Strike could not be ignored. King was ready to consider new solutions, even those being spoken about by a growing Left – solutions such as old age pensions.

Under his leadership the Liberal party would stand tall in the world. King had developed important American bonds, which could help develop Canadian interests south of the border. His experience overseas and in Britain left him eager to see Canada counted in the international community. At the last words of his speech, a tumultuous demonstration erupted. The throng of Liberal convention goers was on its feet, applauding madly.

King took his seat, feeling so near his goal that he fairly trembled. He remembered his morning reading in the inspirational book Bella had given him. Emerson's words had prophesied, "Nothing will be impossible unto you. So nigh is grandeur to our dust. So near is God to man. When Duty whispers low, 'Thou must,' Youth replies, 'I can.'"

He dared to breathe more calmly, feeling that somehow all the others gone on before – Father, Mother, dear Bella, and even Grandfather – were close at hand. Soon the call of God would be answered and the struggle of the common people would be his fight as never before. When the votes were tallied, Laurier's mantle would fall on him.

∽

Laurier House, Ottawa
December 6, 1921
"Oh Rex, you shouldn't have!" Joan Patteson exclaimed. Older than her friend by four years, Joan was fifty-something and wore a stylish yet matronly coiffure. Her brown eyes glowed as she read aloud the inscription on the delicate bracelet.

"To M.J.P. from W.L.M.K.
A strength was in us from the vision
The Campaign of 1921."

"I hardly deserve this," Patteson protested, handing the bracelet over for her husband, Godfroy, to inspect.

"Oh my yes," King disagreed gently. He had met Joan and her bank-manager husband several years before, when they were neighbours in the Roxborough Apartments. Their friendship had deepened over literary discussions, hymn sings, rambles at Kingsmere, and quiet evenings like this one. The Pattesons always welcomed him, Joan in particular. Her warm smile, fine mind, and lovely Christian character were much like Mother's, King had discovered. She knew how much he had suffered from the loss of Mother and how Max's latest illness tormented him with worry. Joan had lost a young daughter, Nancy, and knew more about her friend's pain than what he could express.

Over the last few weeks of campaigning, the Pattesons' support had been uplifting. Yesterday's flowers, which had greeted him cheerfully when he arrived home, were only one of Joan's thoughtful gestures.

"After we hear the results on the radio, what is the first thing you will do as prime minister, Rex?" Godfroy queried.

"*If* I should be prime minister the course of my actions will be decided by Parliament and the people," King answered gravely. "But I know what I shall do when this campaign is over."

"Go to Colorado?" Joan guessed softly.

"Yes," King replied. No more was said. Everyone in the room knew that Max now had muscular dystrophy and it was choking the life out of him. Their next visit, King knew, could be their last. Bella, Father,

Mother, and perhaps Max. King's dreams of being prime minister might soon be met, but who was to share his worries about his strains and stresses? Sister Jennie had trials of her own. Who was to help him measure up to the task of being the most important person in the Dominion of Canada?

The radio crackled alive. The news it would bring would change King's life.

❧

North York, Ontario
September 16, 1922
"Mr. Prime Minister, can you comment on the press release issued from London?" a young reporter called out. Hoping to be the first with the scoop he persisted, "What response will Canada give Britain's invitation to send troops to the Near East?"

King fairly spluttered. He had heard nothing about the statement! Undoubtedly, it had to do with European events at Chanak. Britain wished to limit Turkish expansion in the Dardanelles, an important waterway between the Black and Mediterranean Seas. Headlines like "Turks Attack Christians in Constantinople" and details of the atrocities burned holes in the newspaper daily. However, King had heard nothing about this! How could newspapers be better informed than the Prime Minister's Office? And how could the British government take for granted Canada's commitment to a European military action?

King was fuming, but he kept his burning indignation under control. In a monotone voice he replied,

"That is a question to be decided by the Canadian Parliament."

Fortunately for the new, inexperienced Prime Minister, the tides turned and the Chanak Crisis soon passed. On the point of autonomy, however, King remained unchanged. In March 1923 he sent one of his crack Liberals, Ernest Lapointe, the minister of marine and fisheries, to Washington to sign the Halibut Fisheries Treaty on behalf of Canada. A precedent in Canada's relationship with the mother country was set. No representative of the British Crown was invited.

Laurier House, Ottawa
March 11, 1923
Prime Minister King proudly pointed out to his guests a framed poster on the wall of the third floor hall. The Governor General and his wife, their Excellencies, Lord and Lady Byng, were two of the first official visitors to his new home. "This is the reward of a thousand pounds offered on my grandfather's head," King told them, "by the Lieutenant Governor of Upper Canada, Sir Bond Head."

"Was Bond Head a fool or a wise man?" Lord Byng asked in pleasant provocation.

"Indeed," King chuckled. "I grew up," Willie continued nostalgically, "looking at this picture, dreaming of righting the wrongs against Grandfather's reputation and carrying on his work. Remarkable, isn't it, that less than a century later, the 'scoundrel's' grandson should, as prime minister, have as one of the first guests in his home, His Majesty's representative?" King's blue eyes were merry with the irony of the situation.

"Politics doesn't interest us," Lady Byng sniffed. Lord Byng stood soldier straight. His moustached mouth did not twitch or open to disagree with his wife. "In fact, we shun and detest politics. To change the subject," Viscountess Byng trotted on with her British accent, "let me say that Lady Laurier was very generous to will you this lovely home."

"I am grateful to Lady Laurier. However, politics do not pay handsomely and it is no secret that I could ill afford the work to renovate the house. Fortunately, I have many generous Liberal supporters," King explained. "If we step into the library I can show you some of the fine things Peter Larkin has sent from Britain. Lady Byng, would you care to see the portrait of my mother? And Lord Byng, you might be interested in glancing at some of the works on what I call 'the shelf of the humble,' the books written by my grandfather, my father, my brother, and myself."

King and his guests concluded the tour and returned to take tea in the dining room. The conversation centred on the Byngs' admiration for the lovely furnishings sent by Larkin, the Salada tea magnate, King's benefactor and Canadian high commissioner to London. Talk of Britain led Lady Byng to comment on the length of Canadian winters.

"I miss the pipe of the cheeky wren and the little robin redbreast that we heard at home on even the dullest winter days," she bemoaned.

As the dessert tray went round, Byng started talking about his interest in phrenology. He was one of a number of people who believed that examining the shape of someone's head could "scientifically" tell them about that person's character. Phrenological diagrams divided the head into certain areas, and practitioners only had to feel someone's head to know whether they were cautious, secretive, spiritual and so on. Byng was very interested in the size and number of bumps on the heads of King's ministers.

King was glad politics were not a topic of conversation. As the new leader of the country, he was cautiously learning how to manoeuver in Parliament. He tried to balance the needs of his constituents in North York and those of his own party. He wanted both to woo the errant Union Liberals and Progressives back to the Liberal party while doing as much damage as was civilly possible to his "worthy" opponent, the Conservative leader and former prime minister, Arthur Meighen. King had previously met Meighen on the debating floor at university. Today, as political adversaries, the two cordially despised each other.

When King was not working, he found it pleasant to relax in the golden-bricked security of his Sandy Hill home. The antiques around him whispered stories of the past. The portraits on the walls watched over him: Sir Wilfrid and Lady Laurier, Gladstone, Mother and Father, his grandmothers and Grandfather. On the mantel of the bedroom fireplace, the vigil was kept by the photographs of his dead siblings, sister Bella and recently deceased brother Max.

Although Lady Byng poured the tea, the real presence presiding in the sombre-panelled dining room was the portrait of Mother. Lady Byng felt a sense of family at Laurier House, although the family was alive only on canvas and celluloid. Approving looks came from painted eyes. Encouragement smiled on sepia-toned lips.

"Are you not lonely here, Mr. King?" Lady Byng queried.

"I should ask for nothing more than to be married," King replied frankly. "But alas, such joyful domestic circumstances continue to elude me. I am, though, quite happy to have a home."

He was home, but since Max's painful and tragic death less than a year ago, more than ever Willie was alone. He was thankful the affairs of the nation demanded his attention and took up long hours, six and a half days a week. If he could, he would work even longer and harder to serve the people, to succeed in doing God's will. And somehow he felt that Mother, Father, Bella, Max, and even Bert and others were nearby, pushing him on. "And I must confess," he added, speaking in Lady Evelyn's direction, "I never feel them far away. It's almost as if they are trying to communicate with me."

"Well, Mr. Prime Minister," Lady Byng responded with a glance in her husband's direction, "there are many ways in which it is possible to communicate with the spirits of those who have departed. There are, in fact, many well-born and educated people, such as yourself, who know this. There are even guides who can help research."

Lord Byng cleared his throat uncomfortably. The study of bumps on heads was different from psychical research.

"Perhaps we can speak about this at another time," Lady Byng concluded before sailing off on a description of her rock garden.

∞

London, England
September 23, 1923
King felt he usually looked flabby. He was, in some ways, meek and fuddling in appearance: a dumpy middle-aged man in a drab, grey suit, a shank of hair pulled stiffly across his forehead to hide his balding pate. For the Imperial Conference in London in 1923, King had been shopping. The prime minister of Canada had a new look to present to the world.

His eyes shone blue-jay bright. A shiny black top hat sat firmly on his head. Striped trousers, white shirt, collar, vest, handkerchief, tie and tie pin were all carefully chosen. Swinging his cane and looking like a man in a hurry to complete a mission, he stepped smartly across the pavement. The business of the Dominion of Canada was singularly on his mind.

King was ready to begin the weeks of meetings of an Imperial Conference that would see an important shift of thinking. Canada, under King's administration, would no longer instantly obey Britain's orders – at least, not before parliamentary consultation occurred to determine her best interests. And this was only a first peek at the changes that needed to come.

∞

Prime Minister's Office
East Block, Parliament Buildings, Ottawa
June 29, 1926
Part of King wanted to crumple the letter furiously.
The Governor General had refused the advice of his
prime minister. Despite King's eloquent and well-rea-
soned request, Lord Byng refused to sign the Order-in-
Council dissolving Parliament in order to call an elec-
tion!

The election of September 1925 had produced no
clear majority. The Conservatives possessed 116 seats,
the Liberals 101, and the Progressives the decisive 24.
Although he had lost his seat, King, supported by some
members of his party, decided to continue as prime
minister on the condition that he could obtain a vote of
confidence in Parliament. If the Progressives would
support the Liberals' bills, King would be able to govern.

When a seat was found for him in a by-election in
Prince Albert, Saskatchewan, and a positive vote
secured in the House of Commons, King became the
first Canadian prime minister to head a minority government. Daily he sweated a dainty step on the
tightrope between presenting policy pleasing to the
Progressives and policy acceptable to his own party.
Yet, a bill to set in motion the federal/provincial
machinery for an old age pension was not enough, and
the tightrope snapped. A Customs scandal involving
alcohol smuggling caused some of the Progressives,
such as an agonized Agnes Macphail, to doubt the government's innocence and moral integrity. The Liberals'
crucial support was slipping away.

The debate over four days and nights could not resolve the issue, and it was clear that King's government was coming down. Before he was pushed too far, King snapped back up, eager to have Parliament dissolved in order to hold an election and gain a secure majority. He was refused! The Governor General had initiated a constitutional crisis unprecedented in the history of Canada!

Since Byng would not adhere to the constitution and dissolve Parliament as his prime minister requested, the prime minister had taken another line of action. To everyone's surprise he had resigned.

King reread Governor General Byng's letter accepting his resignation.

> Gov't House
> Ottawa
> June 29th, 1926
> My dear Mr. King,
>
> I must acknowledge on paper, with many thanks, the receipt of your letter handed to me at our meeting yesterday.
>
> In trying to condense all that has passed between us during the last week, it seems to my mind that there is really only one point at issue.
>
> You advise me "that as, in your opinion, Mr. Meighen is unable to govern the country, there should be another Election with the present machinery to enable the people to decide." My contention is that Mr. Meighen has not been given a chance of trying to govern, or saying that he cannot do so, and that

all reasonable expedients should be tried before resorting to another Election.

Permit me to say once more that, before deciding on my constitutional course on this matter, I gave the subject the most fair-minded and painstaking consideration which it was in my power to apply.

I can only add how sincerely I regret the severance of our official companionship, and how gratefully I acknowledge the help of your counsel and cooperation.

With Warmest Wishes,
Yrs sincerely, Byng of Vimy

King came to a realization. *Let the Governor General give Meighen his chance to govern*, he decided almost gleefully. *Let Meighen inherit the problems of the West and more!* King would sit back while keeping one eye open for an opportunity. When the chance came, he would seize it. The country needed an election to let the people show that they wanted to end autocracy. He would go forward with the strength of God and His Might and Right to battle as his forefathers battled for the rights of the people – and God's will on earth. Already ideas were booming into his mind like thunderclaps. Grandfather's war for the rights of the many against the wishes of the powerful few in government, was not over – not yet.

∽

Liverpool, England
October 17, 1926
King descended the ship's gangplank, his face set in a determined smile. Once again he was in England to attend an Imperial Conference in London as Canada's prime minister and secretary of state.

Meighen's government had lasted three days. King had quickly swept it out of the way with a trap of technical questions that had led to a vote of confidence. Before Meighen could take office, he had to satisfy the curious dictates of the day, which said that ministers must be re-elected before assuming office. While Meighen was out of the House seeking re-election, King descended on his unprotected ministers one by one. His relentless questioning ascertained that none had taken an oath as minister of the Crown but were merely acting ministers. These men, King revealed, were not "entitled to spend one five-cent piece of the public money." The ensuing clamour in the House led to a federal election. Meighen lost, and the Conservatives slipped to 91 seats. The Progressives held 12, the United Farmers of Alberta (U.F.A.) 11, and several seats went to Labour and Independents. The Liberals garnered 116 seats, and an additional 10 seats were won by the Liberal-Progressives. King had a firmer mandate to rule. *Chosen by the people. Chosen by God.*

Only two weeks after the fatiguing election he had boarded the ship for England. In some ways King had not been able to prepare for the conference, but in others he was more than ready. The conference of 1923 had seen a shift in attitudes. Now King firmly intended to steer the other delegates toward voting for recommendations of constitutional equality with a clearly defined role for the Governor General.

Canada had grown up and was now more than capable of regulating her national affairs on her own. She also had her ideas about international issues, and these were sometimes different from those of the mother country. When the Balfour Report defined the dominions as autonomous and equal in status, it was clear that the Colonial Era, as it had been known, was over. An age of partners in a Commonwealth was beginning, and Canada and her sister nations considered themselves equal partners.

When the endless meetings, official engagements, and necessary tea appearances were finished, King planned to do some private visiting. He had some questions of his own that he had to investigate. Questions about the past and the future, that only people like scientist and well-known British spiritualist Sir Oliver Lodge could answer.

Laurier House, Ottawa
July 3, 1927
"At work already I see?" King asked, joining his guest.

"Yes, I'm doing a map of my route" the tall, slim young man replied casually. Charles Lindbergh, the American aviation hero, had bravely completed the first nonstop transatlantic flight in May. Now he was the star of Canada's Diamond Jubilee birthday celebrations. "I must say, that was some day yesterday! Landing here in Ottawa, then the ceremonies, the visits, the receptions, the champagne. You Canadians sure know how to celebrate! Oh! That reminds me, here are your studs. Thank you for the loan."

"Mrs. Patteson gave those to me. Perhaps she noticed you were wearing them at the party here yesterday evening. She would have been honoured. By the way, Mrs. Patteson told me that she has heard wonderful reports of the entire celebration. The newspapers said sixty thousand were at Parliament Hill on Friday to see the dedication of the Carillon. Did I tell you," King confided, "that the first impression of the Carillon bells was almost ruined? An aeroplane circled near the Peace Tower, making a frightful noise!"

Lindbergh smiled and then bowed his head as his host said grace.

"Nonetheless," King went on after the prayer, "Governor General Viscount Willingdon and I said our inauguration speeches and the clock was started exactly at noon." King glanced at his guest, but the significance of the auspicious moment seemed unappreciated by the young man.

"I ordered the clock started exactly at noon, with both hands pointing straight up," King explained. He paused and looked at Lindbergh again.

At a loss, Lindbergh sipped his tea.

"The great feature of the day was the radio broadcast across the nation and even as far as Brazil, I'm told. Never before has the human voice been heard at the same time by so many people. I feel it is the beginning of Canada's place in the world, as a world power." He chuckled, "And the next day you arrived – like a young god from the skies in human form!"

Lindbergh looked uncomfortable, but with his mouth full of eggs, he could say little.

"I thank Providence that I could be in office for this occasion. I think I'll make a book of some of the wonderful messages given," King mused. "The only thing that marred it was the death of that young pilot yesterday."

"I must agree," Lindbergh replied cautiously, "with his flight instructor. Johnson was trying to be a little too ambitious."

"Perhaps. Nonetheless, it is a tragedy, and before church I will see that the arrangements for a proper military funeral have been made. And you sir, what are your plans today?"

"I'd like to catch up on my correspondence."

"You must use my library. And if you happen to be writing to your mother give her my regards and tell her I am most interested to hear that we might have a Mackenzie family connection!"

"I will, and thank you for the use of your library. It will inspire…" but before Lindbergh could finish there was a scuttle-clicking on the floor.

"Look who smells sausages!" Lindbergh remarked as a little Irish terrier bounded into the room.

"Sit, boy!" he ordered, rewarding the dog with a piece of sausage.

"Colonel, you'll encourage his bad manners," King admonished in a mock serious tone. "But I must say, I give the little scoundrel the occasional tidbit too, don't I, Pat?" Pat streaked over to King, and sat expectantly with his tail thumping furiously. He received another savoury treat and a warm pat from his master.

Outside the window, the prosperity of summer

stretched lazily down the street, over the city and across the province. For her sixtieth birthday, the whole nation seemed to be unified.

At Laurier House, a good mood scampered around the room like a well-fed dog with a wagging tail. Only the happiness of the moment mattered.

No one saw the shadow of the rain clouds creeping across the lawn.

Ernest Lapointe introduces "Our Leader" with cheers
at the 20th Anniversary of King's Liberal leadership.

A little group at Kingsmere: Godfroy Patteson, Etta Wriedt,
Joan Patteson, King, and dogs – Pat and his brother, Derry.

6

Valley of Shadows

Laurier House, Ottawa
July 26, 1930

K ing entered the room, strode over to the marble statue of his mother, and firmly kissed her lips. "Well, sweetheart," he whispered, "We've done our part."

He had finished campaigning across the West and through Ontario and had just come in from Renfrew today at six o'clock. He was fatigued from speaking in arenas so large they swallowed up his words but somehow did nothing to lessen the volume of the jeers from the unemployed. The thought sustaining him was that Mother never seemed too distant, an angel guiding him from afar. He received confirmation of this in messages from a Kingston fortuneteller, Mrs. Bleaney. Her visions from the spirit world and interpretations of his dreams had helped him since the campaign of 1921. Now Bleaney prophesied victory in the 1930 election even though King worried that his speeches lacked the fire of other campaigns.

Later tonight King would give a coast-to-coast radio broadcast right from the dining room of Laurier House! He was pleased that as he addressed the nation, the paintings of all those he loved most dearly and to whom he owed the most would be about in that memorable and sacred spot in his home: Grandfather, the grandmothers, dear Father and Mother, Mr. Larkin, and Sir Wilfrid Laurier.

The leader of the Opposition would also have his turn to speak. From a political and business point of view, Westerner R.B. Bennett headed as stupid a lot of men as King had ever seen. They'd be better off remaining silent than making promises they couldn't keep. Another of the damnable features of the Tory campaign was their attempt to injure King by making much of his connection to Rockefeller and his absence from Canada during the war. Worst, the Tories suggested that the prime minister had become calloused to labour's cause. "Hypocritical," King pronounced. But he also knew that he had set himself up for such criticism.

He had made one slip. Only one slip. However, the prime minister cannot make even one slip.

Upstairs, as he prepared to take a nap before the broadcast in hopes of getting rid of his splitting headache, King remembered his error.

On April 3 he delivered a speech on unemployment to the House of Commons. He had worked on the speech until 4 a.m., and it met with a standing ovation from his confreres.

Then the Tory harassment had begun, provoking him until he said something that could be totally misrepresented. Although King was clear in his mind that he had been addressing federal/provincial roles and responsibilities, it looked as if he had said the federal government would not give any money to any province headed by a Conservative government.

King recalled saying "I would not give a cent to a Tory government."

"Shame! Shame!" the Opposition cried.

As he lay on his bed, the thudding pain behind his eyes increased. He was not unsympathetic towards the disadvantaged, but technically unemployment was a provincial, not a federal problem. And while there seemed to be increased unemployment with the temporary economic slump precipitated by the Wall Street crash, there was no statistical evidence that showed an emergent national problem. Nor had any provincial premier stepped forward to request emergency assistance. There was, in fact, no reason to open the federal treasury.

I would not give a cent to a Tory government.
Shame! Shame!

The words still rumbled like boulders over his brain.

That regrettable remark, combined with the disorganization of the party machinery and a weak stance on the issue of importation of New Zealand butter, had meant King had to work extra hard at the campaign. At an exhausting pace he had thundered to the West and back with his lieutenant, Québécois Ernest Lapointe.

One of the few moments of peace had been at dawn yesterday as the train passed through Kitchener. King remembered the town when it was called Berlin. He grew excited when, in the half dark, he thought he saw a familiar white gate. "Wake up!" he had cried to his travelling companion. "That's Woodside! That's where I was a boy. Such a happy boyhood," he'd gushed as the pines and poplars whizzed by, "the basis for my present position." Once a boy from Berlin had dreamed of being the prime minister of the Dominion of Canada. "Most of my dreams have been realized," he had murmured.

"With the exception of my sister, Mrs. Lay, my family is gone now," King had informed his seatmate. He had looked out the window at the shadows pierced weakly by the day's new sun. "Only somehow," he'd added, "it feels as though they are quite near by, guiding me."

Now, the memory of their voices quieted the other cries in his head. "*Shame! Shame!*" softened into the sh-sh-sh of the wheels on the track, and for a few minutes, King fell back to dream.

∞

East Block, Parliament Buildings, Ottawa
July 29, 1930
"I would like to extend my sincere congratulations, Mr. Bennett."

King watched as Bennett sat down on the sofa. He looked fatter and flabbier than King had remembered.

"I am glad that the contest is over and that we remained civil," King told his rival. "I must say, however, I regret the personal comments about the war period when I was looking after my family."

"I wasn't in the war either," the new prime minister confessed. Bennett, who was also a bachelor, had different reasons for not enlisting. "I'm missing two toes. Besides, Borden said he needed me at home."

As the conversation turned to the details of handing over the reins of power, King found himself realizing that he was glad to throw onto Bennett's shoulders the need to find a solution for unemployment. He guessed the man would go to pieces from the strain. There were, the former prime minister sensed, more difficult times to come. His party had achieved a fine record of government. When the Tory period ended, surely the Liberals would have a long lease of power.

Looking out the window, Willie noticed two little girls on the lawn, playing. King suddenly felt unburdened. Now he would have more time for literature and gardening at Kingsmere. Finally, he would be able to devote himself more fully to his personal investigations of spiritual phenomena.

∞

Laurier House
February 24, 1932
The third floor was totally silent. As instructed, the servants and secretaries left their employer and his two

female guests to themselves. Pat lay outside the door of the book room and growled when anyone came near.

The room, an oversized closet where books and government papers were stored, was darkened with quilts until it was almost black. King, Joan Patteson, a friend named Mrs. Fulford, and the spiritualist Mrs. Etta Wriedt sat on chairs with a silver-coloured trumpet placed on the floor between them.

The small, white-haired medium in a grey silk dress requested sweetly, "Let us speak the Lord's Prayer."

After the four prayed devoutly, Wriedt closed her eyes and slipped into a trancelike state.

King had been very excited a few days before when he had experienced his first seance with Wriedt. Mrs. Fulford, Senator Fulford's widow, had invited him to her Brockville home to see the Detroit medium. King had been astounded at the parade of spirits who had communicated with him through Wriedt's tin trumpet. Grandfather, Sir Wilfrid, Bert, Father, and Mother had spoken to him and answered his questions, there was no mistaking. Just as Lady Byng, Mrs. Fulford and many others had assured him, now he had *proof* that he could communicate directly with those in heaven!

King had immediately invited Wriedt to come to Ottawa. Rex very badly wanted his friend, Joan, to experience the marvels he had witnessed. He was sure that there were spirits waiting to speak to her, too.

A noise from the flared end of the trumpet made the two seekers almost stop breathing. To Joan it seemed like a strange gasping sound, but very feeble. *It's as if a person is emerging from ether*, Joan thought, *or perhaps like a radio before it becomes quite "heated up."* Joan was too frightened to make any observations out loud.

Miraculously, a woman's voice began to speak. It was indistinguishable at first, and then came more clearly.

This is Isabel. Both Willie and Joan felt their breath coming more quickly. *Is Joan Patteson here?*

"Yes, Mrs. King," Joan squeaked, astonished.

I am happy to meet you, at last, the voice went on strongly. *You have done so much for my beloved son. I have long wanted to meet you and thank you. Also, I have good news for you.*

"For me?" Joan asked incredulously.

Your daughter is here. She has grown up and is a beautiful girl. She will speak to you in a minute.

"Oh my!" Joan could hardly bear the elation at hearing the voice of one who had never spoken on Earth. The daughter she missed so much. Then a worried question came to her. "Who looks after her in Heaven?"

Oh, my dear, there is a kindergarten here for little children, Isabel's voice informed. *They are well cared for. We teach them all kinds of wonderful things – and even all about the parents they left behind and who love them on earth.*

Joan felt enraptured. She had always sensed that her lost child was safe and cared for, but it was so wonderful to be certain.

She's named after you, isn't she? Isabel asked.

Joan stiffened. This was incorrect. The child's name was Alison Rose, but the family had called her…

But we call her Nancy, the voice quickly continued.

Joy flooded back through Joan's body. It was her daughter!

Your father and mother will speak to you also. But my time is short. I wish to speak now to my son.

The trumpet rolled across the floor. It stopped, rapping King on the shins. He picked it up.

My dear, most devoted son. You have been so kind to me. I have felt your love, even here.

"Mother?" King asked.

Yes, Billy, it is your mother. Father is here too and Grandfather. They are very proud of you. We are all here watching you. Now here is Grandfather.

King exhaled. A shudder of relief coursed through him.

I am William Lyon Mackenzie. Mrs. Patteson, I am pleased to meet you. A man's voice with a thick Scottish accent came through the trumpet.

"I am pleased to meet you too, sir. I have studied about you in school."

I am honoured! the voice said with surprise. *I lost much in the Rebellion. As my grandson knows, one makes great sacrifices in public life. He works so hard. I worked so hard. But it was different work. These are different times. Time,* the voice reflected, *does not exist over here. I want my grandson to know that I love him and I will always be with him.*

After the séance King took a moment to write up the events of the day. It was so marvellous, he felt, to have such contact, now, during his upsetting period. The Liberal party had been horribly affected by a terrible scandal, one that had sullied King's personal reputation. Funds had been given to the Liberal campaign from people who had benefitted from contracts related to proposed plans to build the St. Lawrence Seaway. It was made to look as if an interested party, the Beauharnois Syndicate, had paid for King's hotel bill during a holiday in Bermuda. Although King was eventually proven innocent, some other Liberals appeared less so. "We are in the Valley of Humiliation," the party leader confessed before the House of Commons. He had promised that all would be set right. Then he took measures to ensure such a charge could never be brought against a Liberal candidate again. He saw that a National Liberal Foundation and office was organized to handle campaign funds and to strengthen the party unity through improved communication. Nonetheless, the taste of disgrace remained bitterly with King.

∞

Patteson Residence
Elgin St., Ottawa
December 24, 1933
King and Joan sat across from each other at a little table. Their hands were placed on its surface palms down, fingers touching lightly. The room was heavy with the smell of Christmas roses, but darkened so that the blooms could barely be discerned. A small light glowed, just enough to illuminate a notepad beside King.

Their fingers began to tap out letters. With his pencil stub, King transcribed *Mother King*.

"Mother," King breathed. "It's Mother."

Mother King gave her love, and then Joan's mother sent the same message. Father King soon appeared.

Father: Happy Christmas. Go to bed early. Eat less.

"Good advice!" King said.

"Quiet, Rex!" Joan commanded.

As the knocks began again, King wrote down each letter and "translated" the jumble into the answers to their questions. Since their minds had been opened to the possibilities of communication with those in the spirit world, he and Joan found that through the little table they themselves could have direct contact without going through a medium. Willie's brother spoke now.

Max: Go to bed early. Let wine alone. Exercise more.

"Should I walk more?" King asked the shadows.

Yes.

"When?"

At night.

Now it was Joan's turn to ask the spirit of Dr. Macdougall King a medical question. "Will Godfroy's hand soon be better?"

Yes.

"Is it cancer?"

No.

The name Laurier was tapped out next.

Learn French. Have someone teach you.

"Does it mean another war?" King queried.

Yes.

"Do you know how soon?"

The spirits thought a war might come in the reign of Edward VIII. As King George V was currently on the throne, this caused Joan to ask if they had "knowledge of the future." The answer was: *Yes.*

King's heroes, the British prime minister Gladstone and his own rebel grandfather William Lyon Mackenzie, were among those who joined in the talk and gave political advice.

Gladstone: Strive valiantly.

Mackenzie Lyon: I will help you.

Blake: Go slowly dealing with Bennett.

Message from all: Keep up your courage.

They tapped until the spirits told them to *go to bed* late Christmas Eve.

Making his way home to Laurier House, King felt the cold of the night. He was aware that a record number of people on relief were suffering – one million in a country of nearly ten million. Many of these hungry men, King knew, were unhappy that Bennett had not kept his election promises of ending unemployment. They were desperately looking for answers outside of traditional political means and were turning to new theories and parties.

King too, was looking for answers in new ways, but to different questions. Preparing for bed, he thought of the Christmases at Woodside – the way he or Max or Father had dressed up as Santa. Perhaps thinking about them just now meant something. Perhaps he would see his father or Max in a vision while he slept.

Beside King's bed, Pat stirred in his little basket. "I wonder if he's dreaming of the Irish terrier on the

Christmas card that Mrs. Wriedt sent?" King stretched out comfortably, feeling warm and blessed. "I must make a note to thank..."

Soon, both were snoring contentedly while soft shadows flitted about the room.

∞

Kingsmere, Quebec
July 1, 1936
King and Joan Patteson stood on the lawn at the edge of the forest. "I am going to call this the Arc de Triomphe!" he declared, while placing his hand on a tall column.

"To commemorate the election?" Joan asked slyly.

The Liberals had won the October 14, 1935 federal election. Their posters had proclaimed: "Canada Cannot Stand Another 5 Years of Bennett's Broken Promises." The slogan "It's King or Chaos" garnered the lion's share of the votes for the Liberals, with some for the new parties: the Social Credit and the Co-operative Commonwealth Federation (CCF). Bennett had been trounced.

King's Arc de Triomphe, the doorway to the forest, had, a short time ago, held up the stone walls of the British North American Bank Note Building in Ottawa. Upon hearing that the building was scheduled for demolition, he had purchased the pillars and had them brought to Kingsmere. Over the years he had enlarged his estate to just over two hundred improved hectares and several cottages. A few years before, he had begun adding pieces of other people's cast-off buildings, cobbling together "ruins." He was quite pleased with the effect. Kingsmere looked as grand as any old estate in Britain. The latest addition, this portico, to a part of the forest he called Diana's Grove, was especially inspiring.

"The Arc de Triomphe," he wrote in his diary on July 3rd, commemorated "the place of victory and triumph of July 1, 1936, and all that has led up to that moment, and which marks it as a place of new beginning." He was proud of the civic beautification projects begun in Ottawa. There was also the success his minister of labour had achieved in closing the relief camps after finding work for the unemployed men with the railway. And importantly, there was the work that he had accomplished in Geneva at the League of Nations to encourage cautious peace at a time when Ethiopia, the Rhineland, and Spain were feeling the effects of war.

∞

The Official Residence
Berlin, Germany
June 29, 1937
Hitler was speaking. The prime minister of Canada, waiting for the translation, watched his face with fascination. *His face is much more prepossessing than his pictures would give the impression of,* he noted. *It is not that of a fiery, over-strained nature, but of a calm, passive man deeply and thoughtfully in earnest. His skin is smooth; his face does not present lines of fatigue or weariness.*

Hitler rested his hands on his lap, his eyes fixed on King. *Those eyes,* King decided, *are what is most impressive. There's a liquid quality about them which indicates keen perception and profound sympathy.*

Hitler was explaining to King how he spent most of his time at his country home. "I need quiet and nature to help me think out the problems of my country."

"Very wise," King agreed.

When King was in London at the Imperial Conference and the Coronation of King George VI earlier in the spring, he had been approached by Ribbentrop, the German ambassador. The Canadian prime minister had seized the opportunity for an interview. As senior statesman in the Commonwealth, he wanted to communicate to Hitler that the British Prime Minister, Neville Chamberlain, understood that Germany had an interest in some economic expansion in Eastern Europe. King also hoped to convince Hitler of the necessity of continuing peace.

The Canadian outlook, King told the German leader, would be decided by the Canadian Parliament. "Canada is as free and independent a country as Germany itself, but we feel our freedom is secured in a large part by our being a part of the British Empire." King emphasized "that if that peace is threatened by an aggressive act of any kind on the part of any county, there is little doubt that all parts will resent it."

When the interview concluded, Hitler took in his hands a red square box with a gold eagle on its cover. "Take this," the translator told King, "in appreciation of your visit to Germany."

King opened the box. Inside was a signed picture of Hitler in a beautiful silver frame. *Hitler is such a nice, sweet man*, he thought. *He has many fine qualities, such as devotion to his mother and the ability to rise from limited opportunities through self-education.* King felt sure Hitler was deeply mystical, following his star of destiny as he pursued his goal of freeing his country from tyranny. *I cannot,* King reminded himself, *abide Nazism – the regimentation – the cruelty – the oppression of Jews, but*, he prophesied mentally, *Hitler, the peasant, will rank some day with Joan of Arc among the deliverers of his people.*

"Thank you for the gift," King said to his host "and for the privilege of the interview. I strongly agree with seeking to do greater good for those in humble walks of life and would like to speak more with you about the constructive side of your work. I wish you well with your efforts to help mankind."

Hitler returned to the pressing matters of his dictatorship, while King was free to enjoy being a tourist. He was to meet with members of the youth movement and later go to the opera. But now, he wandered to the far side of the Tiergarten, until he was at the house where he had lived for one season as a student thirty-seven years ago.

The birds sang in the trees overhead, *rejoicing*, King thought. *This is why I was born in Berlin, over sixty years ago in 1874. So that today I could deliver an important message of peace.*

Addressing the Canadian troops in Britain, 1941.
General McNaughton stands by.

7

Holding the Pillars Together

The Gazette, Montreal, March 21, 1939
Canada at War if U.K. Attacked:
Premier King

At Ottawa members of all parties joined
in an attack on German policies. Prime
Minister King, defining the Government's
attitude toward the Empire in time of war,
declared the Dominion would consider it an
act of aggression on the whole Commonwealth if Britain were to be attacked.

Packed galleries and a largely attended
House listened to a carefully prepared statement from the Prime Minister who declared

that any act of aggression against Britain would bring prompt and determined action from the Dominion; that while this was a time for preparedness it was also a time when every avenue of conciliation should be explored.

The Gazette, Montreal, March 23, 1939
Spirits Advise Medium in Verdun The World Faces Seven Years Woe

Unless "Lord Kitchener and a man named Gladstone" were blowing sour notes on their spirit trumpets last night the world is scheduled for momentous changes during the next seven years, according to prophecies voiced "through" the Rev. Mary Ellen Goodling, pastor of the Holy Trinity Temple of Light, East Preston Street, Baltimore, Md. at a meeting of the congregation of the Verdun Progressive Spiritualist Church.

Madame Goodling predicted: The return of Edward VIII to the throne he abdicated; the permanent residence of the King and Queen in Canada, which would become the centre of the Empire; "seven more years of Hitler"; and the break up of the British Empire as it is known today.

Her plump figure draped in a flowing gown, her round face hidden by a veil, a gold cross hanging on a chain from her neck, the "prophetess" presented a living picture of the "White Sister" as she began her forecasts at the beginning of a period given over to "messages."

As though in a trance and speaking in a quick, smooth, lulling voice, Mrs. Goodling told the gathering that she was "moved by some force" to proclaim the prophecies.

∞

Royal York Hotel, Toronto
August 8, 1939
King leafed through the banquet program.

Complimentary Banquet
Tendered to
Rt. Hon. Mackenzie King
By the Liberal Party of Canada
On the Completion of Twenty Years of Continuous
Leadership
1919-1939

Menu
Celery Queen Olives
Fruit Cocktail
Grilled Chicken Maître D'Hotel
Green Peas

His eyes stopped. *Green Peas. I hate green peas.* To King it seemed that everything about the day had been perfect. Despite the storm clouds of war drawing ever nearer, Liberal supporters had made this his day. The whole thing was delightful – except for the peas. If he had been in charge of the details, this oversight would never have occurred.

King read the Toast List. The twenty-first speaker, the Honourable Cairine Wilson, was giving her tribute. Wilson represented one of the important changes since King had become Liberal Leader. She was the first woman appointed to the Canadian Senate and the only one listed on the Roll Call pages of Liberal members in the cabinet, House of Commons, and Senate.

That program section devoted to King's Significant Record listed the Imperial Conferences attended, the four elections won, and the books authored. The article informed readers that "of political leaders in Canada, Sir John A. Macdonald and Sir Wilfrid Laurier alone were leaders of their party for over twenty years."

King thought of some of his happy memories. Such a lovely time he'd had just a short while ago when, during the royal visit, Pat, with his little red bow, had lain at Queen Elizabeth's feet throughout the luncheon at Laurier House.

The confident response he had prepared to Wilson's toast recalled some of the many triumphant moments of his leadership. No one must sense that he was beginning to tire. The question squeezing his stomach was *How will I hold the nation together if war comes?* In March he'd promised the House of Commons "conscription of men for overseas service will not be a necessary or effective step." If once again, as in the First World War, the French interests were pitted against the English, King was sure the country would be torn asunder.

The spirits informed him God had chosen him for a special mission. He would prevent civil war at all costs.

∞

Prime Minister's Office
East Block, Parliament Buildings
Ottawa
September 5, 1939
"Mackenzie," Franklin D. Roosevelt's voice on the other end of the telephone boomed. F.D.R., the American president, was as friendly as usual, but King sensed a slight nervousness. Earlier in the conversation, King had assured Cordell Hull, the American secretary of state, that Canada would not be at war until Parliament met to make a decision.

Roosevelt seemed pleased. It was clear where American sympathies lay, but officially the United States was not supporting any active belligerents in the war. Until Canada's status was decided, America could hurriedly ship planes and guns north. Canadians would help this war equipment make its way over to Europe.

King did not tell the American president, his grandfather had told him a few days earlier that *Hitler does not want to have war.* Nor had Mackenzie *wanted the Rebellion.*

However, five days later Parliament held a Special War Session.

On Sunday, September 10, at the request of his Parliament, King George VI approved the Canadian declaration of war.

∞

Prime Minister's Office
East Block, Parliament Buildings, Ottawa
December 17, 1939
The lights were still burning in the prime minister's office, even though the Peace Tower clock was striking midnight. As the last gong faded away, the door to the office opened. Arnold Heeney, Canada's secretary of the War Committee, rushed in and seized King's hand. "Let me be the first to congratulate you," he said cheerily, before the Governor General and the British Commonwealth and Canadians members of the signing party could add their wishes.

King's "birthday present" was to sign the British Commonwealth Air Training Plan. He felt that the long-negotiated document was to be one of Canada's most important contributions to the war. At Britain's side, Canada provided the mother country with volunteer soldiers, food, and supplies and helped facilitate communications between Britain and the United States. Significant financial commitment and the building of sixty airfields over the next three years would go a long way to boost the training of Commonwealth pilots.

Volunteer soldiers were sailing to Britain, and Parliament might soon need to enact legislation that would mobilize men to protect Canadian shores. Conscription for overseas, the prime minister predicted, would not be necessary. However, King was aware that there were those who were willing to stake more than their reputations on a different path of action.

∞

Ontario Legislature Building, Toronto
January 18, 1940
"Let me say again," Premier Hepburn fixed his intense blue-fire gaze on both his fellow Liberals and the Conservatives, "that I stand firm in my statements that Mr. King has not done his duty to his country – never has and never will." Next, the Ontario premier called for a vote on a resolution "regretting that the Federal Government at Ottawa has made so little effort to prosecute Canada's duty in the war in the vigorous manner the people of Canada desire to see."

The surprise was so great that one could have heard a pin drop, despite the new rose-coloured carpet on the floor of the Ontario Legislature. A provincial Liberal leader turning on the leader of his own federal party!

The unpredictable leader of the Ontario Liberals, Mitch Hepburn, had long felt that the federal government was deliberately stunting his province's growth. He'd already gone on record saying that he was a Liberal, but not a Mackenzie King Liberal. King, he was sure, was personally responsible for blocking the sale of Ontario hydroelectric power to the United States and Canada's lackadaisical response to the war. This was not a time for fence-sitting on the issue of conscription. It was a time for action.

When the results of the vote were added up, the Ontario War Resolution was passed with forty-four votes to ten! Canada, it seemed, was about to tear herself to bits.

∞

Massey Hall, Toronto
March 14, 1940
King felt his eyes misting. *This is the kind of man*, he thought, *my grandfather must have had around him in the Rebellion days. Men who were prepared to endure all kinds of hardship for the sake of the cause and of personal loyalty.*

On stage was Henry Corwin Nixon, the person Hepburn had considered his right-hand man. Not any more. Nixon had arrived at the rally unannounced and told the audience, "My good wife and I just drove down from the farm to be here and to say to you that come what may we are behind Mr. King." Applause rolled across the room like storm waves breaking. It was the turning point in the evening and, King felt, in the federal election campaign.

King had met the challenge of Hepburn's War Resolution by calling a federal election. Up to that time the prime minister had refused to enter the boxing ring of provincial politics. Hepburn and Quebec's premier, Maurice Duplessis, mostly ordered business in their provinces as they saw fit. But the War Resolution was enough to prompt King to order a general election. Winning a strong majority would prove that all across the country the people supported King and the Liberal policies during this time of war.

After a campaign visit to his constituency in Prince Albert, Saskatchewan, King travelled to Toronto, the very seat of the provincial government, to attend a rally of Liberal supporters. Many important men and women gave speeches, including Sir William Mulock, King's longtime friend, who was now aged ninety-six. Ernest Lapointe, the minister of justice and King's strong ally, drew applause when he described King as a man "who has serenity in his soul; who is free of hatred and jealousy." But it was Nixon's declaration of loyalty that brought the house down.

King breathed a sigh of relief. It was an elegant bug-squashing.

On March 26, the Liberals took an overwhelming 184 out of 245 seats. The defeated leader of the federal Conservative Party, Robert Manion, thanked the Leader of the Ontario Liberal Party. "Just a word of appreciation," Manion wrote to Hepburn, "for all you tried to do in our behalf – or at least against the fat little jelly fish out at Kingsmere, but somehow he seems to come out on top."

∞

Kingsmere, Quebec
July 15, 1941
MacLeod, King's personal valet, entered his employer's bedroom. It was time to inject Pat with the stimulant the veterinarian had prescribed. The poor aged animal wasn't going to live for much longer.

King sat on the edge of the bed in his pyjamas, clutching his best friend in his arms. Pat vomited, whined, and struggled to breathe. The prime minister stroked the rough fur of his "dear little chap" and prayed. As MacLeod retreated down the hall, he could hear Pat's master singing:

"Safe in the arms of Jesus, Safe on His gentle breast,
There by his love o'er shaded, Sweetly my soul shall rest."[1]

The drama lasted all night. King was sure that Pat would pass on just after 5 a.m. He'd dropped his watch earlier, and the hands stopped at this time, which Willie felt predicted the time of death. But since dawn MacLeod had not been called. At nearly 8 a.m. he rapped on the door.

"Come in," was the whispered reply.

King lay on his rumpled bed, his hair tousled, dark circles under his eyes. In his arms was the body of Pat. It appeared that he had been holding Pat this way for some time.

"Shall I summon Mrs. Patteson?" MacLeod asked nervously.

King nodded yes. Joan would know what to do. MacLeod withdrew quickly.

"My little best friend I have had – or man ever had – you're gone now. You've bounded in one long leap across the chasm which men call death," King whispered to the nearly cold form. "You've gone to be with your little dog brudder, Joan's Derry and the other loved ones. You'll give them messages of love, won't you Pat? You'll let Father, Mother, Bella, Max, Sir Wilfrid and Lady Laurier, Mr. and Mrs. Larkin, and the grandparents know. And we'll all be together one day soon."

---

1. "Safe in the Arms of Jesus," words by Frances Jane (Fanny) Crosby, 1868.

When Patteson arrived, King was weeping. Who would sit with him as he read the war news, sharing biscuits over a cup of Ovaltine? No one else could offer such quiet camaraderie and love. Who would help him be prime minister in these nightmarish times?

⊙

Aldershot, Britain
August 23, 1941
Clutching his umbrella tightly, King strode to the microphone. A sea of thousands of Canadian soldiers of the First Division looked at him expectantly. As the rain poured down, King mumbled weakly into the microphone.

Some men applauded, some men booed. They couldn't hear, they were wet, they hated politicians. King's speech rambled on. "Speak up, speak up," some men called. Others continued booing while still others clapped approvingly. *Tory tactics*, King thought of the booers and ignored them.

What did they want to hear from a politician, any politician? King sensed that they were tired of waiting around Britain. They'd rather be fighting on the Continent. Inspired, the prime minister shouted into the microphone "I gather from the applause that many of you are impatient and would rather be engaged in more active operations than you are today."

The men cheered.

The press, however, made a front-page story of the "booing incident."

Three days after this incident, when Lieutenant-General A.G.L. McNaughton, commander of the Canadian Corps, asked him without warning to address the troops, King was in agony. He sensed what felt like a dart pierce through his bowels, and he felt quite sick and faint.

What could he tell these fine, vigorous, homesick young men? "Offering their lives," he would tell his diary, "is infinitely greater than anything I myself am called upon to do, except to suffer perpetually from a Tory mob."

Overall, King felt that, as the spirits of Lord Grey, Gladstone, Theodore Roosevelt, and the family had predicted, the trip was a success. It had begun with the wonderful flight over the ocean on a Liberator bomber. When he was a boy Willie had daydreamed while looking at the sky through the branches of the trees at Woodside. At nearly seventy years of age it was a tremendous feeling for him to be near those clouds, knowing his dreams of being prime minister were fulfilled. As night fell, he lay on a comfortable cot covered with the Mackenzie tartan and awaited sleep. He was flying – quite a feat!

When King arrived in Britain, Winston Churchill, the British prime minister, had updated him on war happenings. He spoke about his recent communications with Roosevelt off the shores of the British colony of Newfoundland. Then Churchill had assured his colleague that, although he was glad to have Canadian troops guarding the shores of Britain, overseas conscription hardly seemed necessary. Canada was doing her part as a British dominion.

King knew that in Canada, a mood of conflict threatened to split the nation open. The issue – not one he addressed in his speeches to the Canadian soldiers – was conscription.

∞

The Farm, Kingsmere, Quebec
April 17, 1942
King found solace in one regular ritual. At least once a month during the war he consulted the spirits with Joan. They told him what his dreams meant. They let him know how the war would go. They confirmed he was on the right path with his policies and let him know that they would help.

Father: Good evening. Love to all.

As usual Father was the first to greet them. The rest of the King family, Sir Wilfrid, Gladstone, and others were also regular speakers. And there were new guardians in Heaven.

Pat is leaping wildly with delight, Mother told him, *whenever he hears your name.*

Other voices, recently added, had been familiar ones to King as political colleagues before they had been called to the Other Side. Norman Rogers, the minister of defence, had been killed in a plane crash while en route to a speaking engagement in Toronto on June 10, 1940. King had been breaking the news to Mrs. Rogers when the announcement was made that Italy had joined Germany in the war.

The increasing worry and burden of war had directly contributed to the deaths of some of King's nearest advisers. His chief adviser of foreign affairs, the head of the Department of External Affairs, O.D. Skelton, had died at the wheel of his car, as he suffered a fatal heart attack from a condition worsened by the large amount of work he carried out with the civil service. And the stress of all these announcements had finally made Lapointe succumb to heart problems. On November 29, 1941, a parade of mourners with their heads bowed shuffled silently down the snowy streets of Quebec City. They followed the horse-drawn hearse that carried the body of the big bear of a man who had been King's staunchest supporter in French Canada.

King felt these losses deeply.

What most Canadians did not know was that his personal research gave him hope. It not only confirmed the Christian precept that there is life after death – it proved to him that the human personality survived after death.

After Father opened the seance, Sir Wilfrid came to speak: *I have been doing all I can to get an appreciative vote in Quebec. The clergy are helping in the campaign today.*

King had been forced to take action on the conscription issue. The new minister of defence, James Layton Ralston, had spent considerable time since his appointment on June 5, 1940 campaigning for this end. In fact, he had threatened to resign over what he felt was an unreasonable delay in conscripting for overseas service. King had merely held onto his resignation and as a compromise, arranged for a plebiscite, which was to occur the next day, April 27, 1942. The nation was to vote on whether or not it would release the government from its *promise* of no conscription. The vote would not mean the automatic adoption of the measure.

King worried what the results would be.

Lapointe informed King, *Quebec will be true to you. They will give you a majority in the vote.*

King: "I don't believe that."

Lapointe: You will see that I am right

Rogers: The vote tomorrow will be 80% over the entire nation.

King: "I don't believe that."

The ghosts promised he would *be stronger than ever.* King thought the government might win the vote, but not in Quebec.

How could he go on, he wondered, if only Quebec voted against the plebiscite and Parliament eventually found it necessary to enact such legislation?

Before the spirits said goodnight, they bade him remember that God loved him and had a special mission for him. King knew he must go on.

The next day, although French Canada remained solidly against conscription, the overall results of the plebiscite were in favour of releasing the government from its anti-conscription promise. That night King had another dream. Two stones – like pillars – were in his hands, and he was trying to hold them together. It was up to him to join the French and the English parts in one solid country, and what he was doing seemed to be working.

A message of victory, broadcast from San Francisco, May 8, 1945.

8

The Price of Peace

The Connaught Building, Ottawa
October 19, 1944

"How are you Chubby?" James Layton Ralston, the minister of defence, inquired in a low, growly voice as the maître d' showed the minister of air defence, Charles Gavan Power, to his seat.

"Better than you, it seems!" Power replied, his blue eyes twinkling. "You sound terrible."

"I've got a bad cold," Ralston sniffled, taking out his handkerchief and applying it to his hawkish nose. Even his dark eyes behind his black-rimmed glasses seemed to be running.

Power clucked sympathetically. "Catch that overseas?"

Ralston shrugged.

Chubby ordered a drink. Ralston noted the choice. Power's notorious reputation for alcoholic consumption was strongly disapproved of by the prime minister.

"How was Europe?" Power asked in an upbeat tone. He knew the answer would be less jolly. Ralston had gone to England, Italy, and France to assess for himself the conditions of the Canadian Expeditionary Force. He had returned only yesterday and immediately called Power to request a lunch meeting. The minister of defence sounded so worried and depressed that Power agreed to cancel a previous engagement.

"Bad, things were bad," came the reply. "What I saw was terrible."

As Power quaffed his drink, Ralston shared the bleak picture painted by General Stuart, chief of the general staff. "The casualties are much higher than anticipated. There are just not enough reinforcements, and unless they can be found elsewhere, steps *must* be taken to impose conscription for overseas," he said, shaking his head. "I've already told the prime minister what Stuart concluded."

"I presume," Power anticipated, "he expressed the view that at this time he would not support any move toward conscription."

The minister of defence gave a disgusted shudder. "What is the man waiting for? He's got his plebiscite, the people think they voted for conscription. But what does it mean to King? 'Conscription if necessary, not necessarily conscription' – that's the new motto King's adopted. Plebiscite – schmebiscite – that's what I think!

The Canadian people want action. Well," Ralston added disapprovingly, "except those in Quebec."

A Quebec MP, Power shot Ralston a look, but did not speak except to place another drink order with the waiter. The 1940 National Resource Mobilization Act had created a body of men, the NRMA, sometimes called the Zombies, who were conscripted to serve *in* Canada. The national plebiscite was not about immediately changing their status. It was about freeing the King government from its *promise* only. However, the people of Quebec had voted very strongly against even this measure.

Ralston considered his soup uncomfortably. Then, passionately, he began a new verbal volley, "Chubby, conditions are simply unsupportable overseas. Men who have been wounded two or even three times are being sent back onto the battlefield! They are desperate for replacements, and voluntary recruitment just isn't working. What does King propose? Still nothing. *I* propose that we send 15,000 NRMA troops overseas as early as December."

Now Power took an extra long minute cooling his soup before he spoke. A lieutenant in the First World War, Power had been wounded in September 1916 and returned home, unfit for service. On the wall of his office there was a photo of six young men, including himself, in uniform. Of the six he was the only one to have returned. He summed up his experiences when he told his followers in Quebec: "I went overseas in one war. I returned. I'll never go back, and I'll never send anybody else."

That promise had become very important in the 1939 provincial election in Quebec. Premier Maurice Duplessis called a provincial election to vote on federal issues of conscription and war participation. Duplessis would have tightened his reign on *la belle province* had not the federal Liberals come to the aid of their provincial confreres. Each federal minister – Lapointe, Cardin, Power himself – had promised to resign if conscription was enacted. They convinced the people to support a Liberal government, the only one that held their interests at heart.

Lapointe was dead, and P.J.A. Cardin had already resigned. It was up to Power to keep his word.

"Ralston, you know where I stand," he said with solemn integrity. "And now, tell me," Power requested, changing the subject, "did they have any good wine in France?"

∞

Hôtel-Dieu Hospital, Quebec City
November 12, 1944
"How was the operation? How are you feeling?" Louis St. Laurent, the minister of justice and attorney general, inquired in a concerned voice, as he took a seat beside Power's bed.

"I feel much better with my appendix out than in!" Power chuckled. "Ow!" he winced. "It only hurts when I laugh."

"Be still then, and I'll tell you what's happening."

Power nodded his agreement. St. Laurent had been invited into the King government, in part on Power's recommendation. After Lapointe's death King knew how much he needed topnotch representation in Quebec. The quiet lawyer seemed to fit the bill.

Shortly after his arrival on Parliament Hill, St. Laurent had been forced to give his opinion on conscription. He answered that he had entered cabinet at the request of Mr. King, and would do his duty in whatever King felt necessary during the war. Power felt this was probably the most honest statement by any Québécois in the House. It also left St. Laurent less boxed in than the other parliamentarians from the province.

The patient listened eagerly as the soft-spoken St. Laurent caught him up on the flurry of events that had blown a storm through Ottawa since Power's departure on October 27. St. Laurent described how the shrill cacophony of the pro- and anti-conscriptionists was met by stony silence from the man at the helm of the country. King was sure the war overseas would be over soon. Enacting conscription would unleash the dogs of civil war at home. King still hoped a compromise could be made. When Ralston seemed unable to accept this, King made a move that surprised many.

"On November first, the prime minister 'accepted' Ralston's letter of resignation as minister of defence," St. Laurent informed his colleague.

"Accepted? The letter Ralston tendered two years ago?"

St. Laurent nodded. "Yes, the one from the conscription crisis in 1942. Ralston never withdrew it. King said it was a 'trying thing' to go on in this period with this resignation 'simply held.' He *decided* to accept it now that Ralston did not seem to agree with the position on conscription. Ralston was surprised of course, but he shook hands all round and left the meeting quietly. We were surprised too, but no one else went out the door." St. Laurent looked down at his hands. "We soon enough got back to work, that was all. Ralston wrote a letter of confirmation later on yesterday afternoon. McNaughton will take over."

Power sipped his water, so deeply that his moustache got wet and his rather large nose was almost dipped too. "I'd heard a rumour that McNaughton might replace Ralston if he persisted in his attitude."

"Calamitous," St. Laurent muttered. "Conscription would be calamitous."

"And now?" Power asked.

"Now you need your rest. You need your strength," St. Laurent suggested wisely, "so that you can come back to Ottawa as soon as possible."

∞

Parliament Buildings, Ottawa
November 23, 1944
In what seemed an astonishing flip somersault backwards, King announced that the search for volunteers had not produced enough soldiers, and that indeed, conscription was now necessary! The day before, Ralston's replacement, McNaughton, had admitted that despite the appeals he and King had made, he had not been able to find the 10,000 volunteers needed and had recommended that 16,000 NRMA be sent overseas almost at once. McNaughton also told King privately that the military chiefs of staff were prepared to resign if the measure was not enacted. King now wanted conscription. He wanted to announce the new plans to his closest supporters, his party, and then the

cabinet, before telling the House of Commons and the Canadian people.

King called St. Laurent and then Power to Laurier House for a "quiet talk." He seemed to beg Power to stay with the government. Power agreed King's action was the right step to take, considering the threat of a Palace Revolution, but he could not change his position. Later, Power sent King a note.

He read the same note (which King claimed not to have received) aloud at the caucus meeting.

> My dear Mr. King,
>
> Lest there be any question in caucus as to my stand on the new developments and the changed orientation of government policy, I wish to repeat what I have already said to you, namely, that I am not in sympathy with the policy now proposed and I cannot accept any responsibilities for it.

"As I have previously announced to you personally," he addressed the prime minister, "and to my colleagues, I cannot support the present government in this course."

Caucus was adjourned. Power and King went up alone in the elevator toward the cabinet meeting. "I am sorry that I did not receive your note," King said. Under King's regret, Power thought he perhaps sensed a bit of coldness.

At the cabinet meeting, Power got up, shook the prime minister's hand, and said, "I wish you good luck." Having handed in his resignation, the now former minister of national defence for air and associate minister of national defence took his seat. When the meeting was over, Power left the Parliament Buildings.

King went on to the House of Commons and entered the chamber without his longtime colleague. *All these burdens!* He knew that the spirits tried to ease his cares, by sending him signs or messages through dreams and at the little table. Laurier warned King to take care of his health, saying that conscription had been what *killed me in the end*. They assured him that he was making the right course, with conscription, with Power. The month before, the spirits had told him that *Chubby Power is beyond recall, he is a drunkard, but controls himself for a while, he will last for a time but not for long.* Power, perhaps, but how, he wondered, would the others react to his announcement? The spirits had promised cabinet support. But would there be more abandonments?

Before making his surprise speech that introduced conscription, King did a novel thing. He stood, turned his back to the Opposition, and directed his address to the members of his own party.

With apparent calmness King spoke: "I desire to read to the House an order-in-council which sets forth the policy of the government with respect to the extension of service of NRMA personnel, which order is P.C. 8891, and has been approved by His Excellency the Governor General today."

The order he read extended the National Resources Mobilization and the War Measures Act to give the minister of national defence the authority to send NRMA personnel to "the United Kingdom and/or European and/or Mediterranean operational theatres."

King had finally put the legislation in place to send as many as 16,000 Zombies overseas.

∽

Patteson Residence, Elgin St., Ottawa
December 2, 1944
Sir Wilfrid: The victory has been complete. You have outflanked your enemies at every turn.
King: Have I done the right thing?
Sir Wilfrid: Absolutely. It was the only thing to do. God directed your course. God guided your steps from day to day. God will guide you to the end.
Gladstone: Laurier is right. God is your strength and guide.
Father: Your Mother and Grandfather Mackenzie and my father are all here together. We are proud of you. You have saved Canada from civil war.
Sir Wilfrid: King, you have done for Canada, the greatest service of any man in her history. You have beaten the forces of corruption and high finance. You have dumbfounded your brutal opponents. You have made your place in history for all time. Let your mother speak.
Mother: Dear Joan, don't you think Billy has done well?
Mackenzie: William I am proud of you.
Joan: I thought he was here.
Mackenzie: I am right here beside you, Mistress Patteson. Long ago I led a rebellion. William has prevented one. He has saved many lives and much bloodshed.

*Lapointe: I have been there to guide and direct
your actions. You have done the right thing. Quebec
has faith in you.*

*Skelton: You have saved civil war. You have
ensured the troops being reinforced. You have saved
the break up of the government and of the country. You
have saved anarchy in Canada.*

∞

San Francisco, United States
May 7, 1945
"The War in Europe is Ended! Surrender is Uncon-
ditional!" triumphed the headlines of the *New York Times*.

Reading the news gave King a thrill, although he'd
known for some time before it was printed. Nichol, his
personal valet, had come into his hotel room at seven
o'clock to waken King. "I have an important message,
sir," Nichol said joyously. "The war in Europe is over."

"Thank God," King breathed. He turned on his side
and uttered a prayer of thanksgiving and of rededication
to his fellow human beings. Now life could get back to
normal. A federal election was scheduled to be held at
the end of next month, and readjusting the world to life
after years of war had already begun. King was in San
Francisco to work on the draft charter of the United
Nations. As a senior world statesman he was needed to
guide Canada and the world in their next steps.

Approximately 13,000 conscripted men had gone
overseas. They accounted for sixty-nine out of the
42,000 Canadian deaths.

The price of peace had been great.

9

Shadows Nearer,
The Promise of New Dreams

Laurier House, Ottawa
December 23, 1947

My dear Marilyn:

Nothing, in many years has touched my heart more deeply than the word that came in your letter. I am, indeed, pained to know just how sad you must feel,... and I feel for you all more deeply than my words can begin to express.

King paused in his dictation and directed his secretary, Handy, to enclose a cheque for twenty dollars.

King visits Woodside, his boyhood home. Now, in September 1947, Woodside is the home of little Marilyn Kilbasco.

He hoped the amount would make a real difference to the impoverished eight-year-old recipient. He took comfort from the fact that the girl's poor widowed mother, Mrs. Kilbasco, must be receiving the newly created family allowance benefits.

King had met young Marilyn and her family in Kitchener in September. The Kilbascos were one of the last families to live in Woodside, the home the Kings had once rented. Louis Breithaupt and a committee of Liberals had heard that King's old boyhood home had fallen into terrible disrepair and was to be demolished. They thought that a visit might inspire The Chief to support their plans for saving the property as a memorial.

The old man felt great loneliness and sadness at seeing the place where he had felt warm family love now with almost every window broken. However, the little girl who had greeted him and offered him a flower melted his heart.

Upon hearing that Marilyn's father had died, King felt compelled to offer solace – and to hint at the great life he was sure Mr. Kilbasco was experiencing since he had crossed over.

> You must try, notwithstanding your great loss, to make Christmas at Woodside just as bright and cheerful as you can… While we cannot see God, we have the story of the life of the little Christmas child to let us know what He is like. So I am perfectly sure that your dear father, while taken away from you, has been taken to Heaven where God Himself is and that, though you cannot see your dear father,

he can see you, and that his spirit will be watching over you...

When I was a little boy at Woodside, I found all this very difficult to comprehend, but as I have grown older I have come to believe it more strongly every year, and I might say, almost every day.

So don't think of your father as gone. When you say your prayers, ask him, as well as God, to watch over you, and you will see, by and by, how, in some remarkable way, some way you now can never think of, your prayers will be and have been answered.

Your Christmas card is a lovely one, and I thank you warmly for it. I am sure you selected that particular card because the little picture looked like Woodside in the winter time... I shall keep it and your little letter always.

I am sending you, with this letter, as a little Christmas gift from me to you, a real photograph of you and me, taken on the day of my visit to Kitchener. I had mine framed and took it with me to France, and Belgium, and Holland, and England, and always had it on my desk, on the boat across the ocean both ways as well as in the hotels... It will help you to remember the happy time we had at Woodside and I hope will add to your happiness at this Christmas and always.

It brings with it lots of love from me to you.

Your very true friend,

Mackenzie King

Woodside had hardly left his mind. Often the spirits of Bella, Father, Mother, and Max recalled with him the good times they had there, the beautiful golden days safe in the nest from which he had flown to begin his career. Mother pointed out that although he was *still the boy she knew at Woodside*, so much had happened. In a seance on July 7, 1946, she had told Joan glowingly how *Willie began by trying to help children in the hospital* and then *became a young man living in the slums, trying to help the poor. He then tried to fight for Labour's rights and went into Parliament as the minister of labour*. Her spirit recounted how, following Willie's career all her life, she found he never *lost his sympathy with the common people and their needs. He went to England and fought for the rights of Canada as an equal partner in the British government.*

King agreed with the spirits that he had *avoided Civil War* during the conscription crisis. He was glad to have been re-elected and to see new policies bring betterment to the citizens of his country. Despite the war, life had changed greatly for the nearly twelve million people of Canada these last few years: unemployment insurance had been enacted in 1940; quite recently old age pensions were extended to cover more people; and baby bonuses had been paid to families with children since June, 1946. He could be proud that the State guaranteed people a better quality of life than it had when King began as party leader. In fact, their position had now changed in the world. On January 3, 1947 the prime minister was one of twenty-six people to become citizens of Canada when he received certificate number 001. Canadians were no longer defined as citizens of

Britain. Lastly, he could be satisfied that the way was prepared for the people of Newfoundland to join Canada as her tenth province. In many ways most of the dreams he had had as a young man were now fulfilled.

You have taken the Liberal Party out of the depth and raised it to the heights, Grandfather Mackenzie told him. *Your name will go down in Canadian History, as the one who has done most for Canada. You have done honour to the names you bear.*

The spirits let him know his tasks were not yet completed. They told him that they were working through him still, that he was chosen to do important missions as an international statesman. Hitler, he was informed, was now *in lower hell, chained to eternal suffering.* But new problems threatened the world. When a young cipher clerk working at the Russian embassy in Ottawa brought forward evidence of a Soviet spy ring in September 1945, the spirits applauded King's investigation of the Gouzenko Affair. They said King had exposed *the treacheries of Russia,* but encouraged him to visit Stalin. King was invaluable in dealing with such delicate issues. *You must,* Sir Wilfrid and others told their champion, *stay in office.*

He would try to hold on, but at age seventy-three, he knew it could not be for much longer. He worried that the money, books, and the paintings of himself were not all of the legacy he desired to leave. He excitedly discussed with the spirits ideas for turning over Kingsmere, Laurier House, and Woodside to *all* the people of Canada.

What he really wanted to give the people of Canada were his memoirs. The spirits promised he would be given the strength and the time and urged him again and again to leave the story of his life as an example for others. Only there was so much to tell, and even more to do yet. He worried that he would never complete one more important trip abroad, for the upcoming Imperial Conference.

∞

London, Hotel Dorchester
October 15, 1948
Violet Markham was shocked to see her friend looking so shrivelled, so frail – a "sick" man. However, thinking back to her visit to Kingsmere in July 1939, she realized that even then the cares of office had sucked the vigour from King's body. "Will-power, not health, carried him through the war," she'd concluded. King was, in fact, the only leader to stay in office after the war. F.D.R. had died, and Churchill's party had fallen out of public favour.

This broken man was but a shadow of the person she had met at Rideau Hall, the Governor General's residence in Ottawa, almost forty-three years ago to the day. She would remember it in her memoirs – October 21, 1905, Trafalgar Day in her native England: Her host, Governor General Lord Grey, strode across the drawing room, and trailing behind him was a "pleasant-looking man of medium build, with a round face and abundant fair hair."

"You must meet Mackenzie King," Lord Grey told her, "he will be prime minister of Canada some day."

After speaking with the confident thirty-one-year-old man, she felt her doubts about the surprising prediction diminish. The young deputy minister of labour, like herself, had many hopes of helping and reforming humankind. "A charming young man with all the right ideas" she wrote in her diary.

Markham soon returned to her well-feathered nest in England. She married, but continued her work as a social activist. Her campaigning letters were written on stationery that bore the names "Mrs. James Carruthers" and "Miss Violet Markham." King's activities continued to excite her sense of social justice. She found him intriguing: "his personality might be likened to a set of those Chinese boxes which fit so surprisingly into each other, each box different in size and colour and yet making a perfect whole..." But as their friendship grew over the years, Markham realized that his belief in personal survival after death and the power of communication with those who had passed on was "a line of thought in which I was unable to follow." Rex's spiritualism, Markham decided, was a box unto itself, a special interest for his private time.

She regretted that her friend had never married. As late as the early thirties King's name had been linked romantically with that of his longtime friend, Julia Grant. Grant, Ulysses S. Grant's granddaughter, had married to become Princess Cantacuzène. She had eventually divorced the Prince for his infidelities, but by that time King's passions had decidedly cooled. Markham had long ago determined "the mother-cult stood between him and the normal ties of wife and child, which can humanize and soften the often inhuman job of politics." And the blows rained down. She knew that over the years her friend had suffered. "Few men have been more bitterly attacked or accused of motives more unworthy."

She and Rex passed their time discussing politics. Russia and other hot spots were on their minds – especially King's, as illness had forced him to suddenly withdraw from the conference.

"My own feeling," King told her regarding India or Pakistan becoming part of the Commonwealth, "is that the Commonwealth shall need all the friends they can have in what before long may be a test as to who is to rule the world." In his mind were the voices of F.D.R. and others cautioning him about events in the East and warning that war was coming within the next two years.

There was so much King wanted to say, but his shortness of breath and influenza, combined with the effects of strain and pressure over the years, prevented him from talking much.

"Why don't you, for the time being, forget about politics," Markham suggested. She mentioned the book she was writing and urged him to "dictate a few reminiscences about your home and your childhood." But, she realized even that small effort was impossible. The sands were running out.

"Come to Wittersham," she begged. "Stay for a week. Bring your staff," she offered. When King declined, she tried another tactic. "I'm disposing of my wealth," she explained. "As a matter of fact, getting rid of some of it will decrease my taxes." She paused. "You are my oldest friend and it might be helpful at this moment in tiding over the situation if I give you a sum right now."

"I am deeply touched, Violet," King said, looking into her bird-bright eyes and thinking how little she had changed since that Trafalgar Day so many years ago. It was not the first time the person whom the spirits called *a friend to us all* and *a remarkable woman* had come to his aid financially. In the period prior to the First World War, when he was out of power and before he had gone to work for the Rockefellers, she had insisted he take a monthly income from her.

"I'll give at once," Markham responded cheerfully. "Ah, Rex, this will give me such pleasure. I am so worried and I think this is the time to arrange things." Markham feared greatly she would never see her friend again.

King sensed this and told her, "My dear Violet, I have no fears about the future."

Markham was not the only person discussing matters with the ailing Canadian leader. King George, Nehru of India, New Zealand's Prime Minister Fraser, and Prime Minister Liaquat Ali Khan of Pakistan, were some of the distinguished statesmen who visited.

On Saturday, October 23 King had visits at his hotel from Nehru's sister, Madame Pandit, and Eric Louw, the South African minister of external affairs. Two invited guests, Geraldine Cummins and her assistant Miss E.B. Gibbes, almost did not come. Cummins telephoned to warn the Canadian prime minister that she was suffering from a cold. King encouraged her to come regardless. He wanted to talk to the spirits.

Geraldine Cummins was one of the London spiritualists with whom King consulted in his pursuit of psychical research. He had contacted some of them through an influential woman and friend he had met his university days. The founder of the Victorian Order of Nurses, Lady Ishbel Aberdeen, had sought solace after the death of her husband, a former Governor General of Canada. The mediums she found employed automatic writing – going into a trance and writing down what they believed was dictated to them from the spirit world. Thrilled with this new proof of spiritual survival, King met with some of the London contacts whenever he could during the war and after.

Cummins had met King when he had come to England for the wedding of Princess Elizabeth in 1947. At the sitting, Cummins had gone into a trance, her left hand covering her closed eyes while her right hand wrote on the paper her secretary, Miss Gibbes, put in front of her. The words were dictated from her control, called "Astor." Later, Cummins was surprised to find out that King was not a clergyman as she had thought but the prime minister of Canada. She told her assistant that he was the "greatest statesmen of our time. A man with such a record is no credulous fool."

This year, Cummins found her client much altered, although his attractive smile, captivating charm, and spiritual integrity remained. His good-humoured face wore the cares of the invalid that she had foreseen at the previous sitting. With a serious expression in her dark brown eyes and thin face, she had warned him then, "You ought to take a holiday – at least six months." But he only laughed, "I haven't taken a holiday in years." Now it was too late.

"Nowadays," their host complained of his fatigue once his guests were comfortably seated, "statesmen have to fly about the world instead of staying at home doing constructive work directing affairs."

Once Cummins began, she wrote what Astor said for fifty minutes. F.D.R. again urged attention be given to the Far East, warning of war in two years' time. F.D.R. and then Sir Wilfrid encouraged him to stay in office as long as he could. *You alone can manage the numerous conflicting interests in the world*, he told his once young, now aged protégé.

Prime Minister King found the talks as reassuring as usual. "Remarkable," he told Cummins, "just what I wanted."

To himself he wondered how he would find the strength to go on. In April 1948 he would exceed twenty-one years in office and break the record set in the 1700s by Britain's Sir Robert Walpole. Once past 7,619 days King would have held power longer than any other elected statesman in the English-speaking world. Perhaps he would plan to announce his retirement soon after, and perhaps even steer the party toward selecting St. Laurent as leader.

∽

Laurier House, Ottawa
May 19, 1950
Father: Let Grandfather speak.

Grandfather: The doctor will show you what to do. Mother is here. Let her speak

Mother: Dear Willie it is a long time since we had a talk. Joan, I thank you for coming to see Willie each night. I want him not to be concerned about his health. He will be strong again in a short time. Let Max speak.

Max: Don't be concerned about the morphine, you will be rid of it in a short time. Let Bella speak.

Bella: You are going to be strong again. Good night from all.

This is the last recorded seance of Rex, Joan, and friends.

∞

July 21, 1948
Telegram to:
Mrs. James Carruthers
Moon Green
Wittersham
Kent (England)
Our friend's condition has taken serious turn will keep you informed.
Joan

∞

The Farm, Kingsmere, Quebec
July 22, 1950
"Thank you," King whispered to the nurse. He closed his eyes and one last time, went to dream.

W.L.M. King named all his dogs "Pat." The first Pat
– King's "best little friend" – lived for 17 years and
died on 14 July 1941. Pat the second was acquired
in 1941 but died only 6 years later in 1947.
Pat the third was acquired in the mid-40s.

Epilogue

Clipping found in King's diary.
    "The Little Dog Angel Diary" by Norah Holland
from *Spunyarn and Spindrift*.
    High up in the courts of heaven today
    A little dog-angel waits
    With the other angels he will not play,
    But he sits alone at the gates;
    "For I know that my master will come," says he;
    "And when he comes, he will call for me."

Family memories.
Bella, Isabel, Willie, and John King.

"Mother" and "Father." Isabel and John King
with William Lyon Mackenzie King.

Chronology of William Lyon Mackenzie King (1874-1950)

Compiled by Lynne Bowen

KING AND HIS TIMES	CANADA AND THE WORLD
	1791 John Graves Simcoe becomes first governor of Upper Canada; his attempts to create an aristocracy will lead eventually to the formation of the so-called Family Compact.
	1793 In Upper Canada, Governor Simcoe orders a small town to be laid out at the site of Fort Rouillé and names it York.
1795 William Lyon Mackenzie (maternal grandfather) is born in Dundee, Scotland.	

William Lyon Mackenzie King

1805
In Upper Canada, Mennonites from Pennsylvania purchase land and establish the German-speaking settlement of Berlin.

1809
Louis-Joseph Papineau is first elected to the Assembly of Lower Canada; he emerges as the leader of a group of young nationalists known first as the *Parti Canadien* and later as the *Parti Patriote*.

1814
John King (paternal grandfather) is born at Tyric in Aberdeenshire, Scotland.

1820
William Lyon Mackenzie arrives in Upper Canada.

1824
The *Colonial Advocate*, published by William Lyon Mackenzie, is the leading voice of the Reform movement; Mackenzie moves to York.

1828
Mackenzie is elected to the Upper Canada House of Assembly; he will be expelled for his attacks on the ruling Family Compact and be re-elected repeatedly.

1832
Osgoode Hall, the headquarters of the Law Society of Upper Canada, is completed; it will later be

KING AND HIS TIMES	CANADA AND THE WORLD
	expanded to house law courts and the Osgoode Hall Law School.
1834 Mackenzie is elected the first mayor of Toronto.	**1834** In Upper Canada, York is incorporated as the city of Toronto.
	In Lower Canada, Papineau campaigns to force the British government to grant independence to French Canadians.
	1835 Sir Francis Bond Head becomes Lieutenant Governor of Upper Canada.
1836 Mackenzie fails to win re-election to the House of Assembly.	
1837 Embittered by his electoral defeat, Mackenzie leads a poorly conceived revolt; he escapes to the United States (U.S.).	**1837** Queen Victoria assumes the throne of Great Britain and the Empire. Rebellions in Upper and Lower Canada; Papineau flees to the U.S.
1838 John King participates in the Battle of the Windmill.	**1838** In November, British troops and local Canadian militia prevent the invasion of Upper Canada by American troops and Canadian rebels in the Battle of the Windmill near Fort Wellington.
	1841 The Act of Union unites Upper and Lower Canada as equals; together Canada West and Canada

William Lyon Mackenzie King

KING AND HIS TIMES	CANADA AND THE WORLD
	East, as they are now called, form the Province of Canada.
1843 John King (father) is born.	
Isabel Grace Mackenzie (mother) is born in New York State, where her mother and siblings have joined her father in exile.	
	1845 Having been granted amnesty, Papineau returns to Canada East from exile in France.
	1848 Potato famines in Ireland and a series of European rebellions send waves of immigrants to North America.
1849 Mackenzie is pardoned and returns to Canada; he is elected to the Legislative Assembly and continues to work as a journalist.	
	1858 Ottawa is chosen as the capital of the Province of Canada.
1861 Mackenzie dies in Toronto.	
	1867 Canadian Confederation unites Ontario, Quebec, Nova Scotia, and New Brunswick; John A. Macdonald becomes the first prime minister and is knighted by Queen Victoria.

KING AND HIS TIMES

CANADA AND THE WORLD

1871
Papineau dies in Montebello, Quebec.

English historian and journalist Goldwin Smith arrives in Toronto.

1872
John King marries Isabel Mackenzie on December 12; they will reside in Berlin, Ontario.

1872
Civil War general Ulysses S. Grant is elected president of the U.S. for a second term in spite of public scandals during his administration.

1873
Isabel "Bella" Christina Grace King (sister) is born.

1873
Having added three provinces (Manitoba, British Columbia, and Prince Edward Island) to Confederation, Sir John A. Macdonald's government is forced to resign over a scandal involving the funding of the proposed transcontinental railway.

1874
William "Willie" Lyon Mackenzie King is born in Berlin, Ontario to John and Isabel King on December 17.

1874
In Britain, Winston Churchill (future statesman) is born.

In Quebec, Wilfrid Laurier is elected to the House of Commons for the first time.

1876
Janet "Jennie" Lindsey King (sister) is born.

1878
Dougall Macdougall "Max" King (brother) is born.

1878
Macdonald returns triumphantly to power in Ottawa and remains prime minister for the rest of his life.

KING AND HIS TIMES	CANADA AND THE WORLD
	1880 William Ewart Gladstone becomes prime minister of Great Britain.
1882 Willie King attends a meeting where Sir John A. Macdonald is speaking.	
	1883 Arnold Toynbee, a British economist and humanitarian, dies at the age of 31.
	1885 The Canadian Pacific Railway is completed.
	Former U.S. president Ulysses S. Grant dies.
1886 The King family rents and moves into Woodside, a large house on 5.66 wooded hectares.	
1888 King has taken on more responsibilities and even looks after his father's business.	**1888** American Jane Addams visits Toynbee Hall, a settlement house in London, before returning to Chicago and establishing a similar facility at Hull-House a year later.
	1889 In Canada, the Royal Commission on the Relations of Labour and Capital describes the new system of worker exploitation or the "sweat shop system."

KING AND HIS TIMES

1891
King moves to Toronto and enrolls at the University of Toronto (U of T) in political science – a relatively new area of study – and economics.

1893
King is awarded the Blake Scholarship and is voted president of his class; on September 6, he begins to keep a journal and will do so for the rest of his life.

1894
King sits at the bed of a dying child; he has conducted religious services and read to the patients at the Sick Children's Hospital in Toronto ever since he came to the city; like his hero, Gladstone, he tries to help the underprivileged.

1895
Protesting U of T hiring policies, King addresses a large crowd of students; he graduates with a Bachelor of Arts, but the U of T refuses to give him a scholarship to study for his master's degree; the University of Chicago (U of C) offers him a scholarship, but family financial difficulties prevent him from accepting it; he decides to work as a tutor and a journalist for a year and study law in the evenings.

CANADA AND THE WORLD

1891
Canada and the Canadian Question by Goldwin Smith is published; the book advocates union with the U.S.

Sir John A. Macdonald dies in Ottawa.

1893
The Earl of Aberdeen becomes Canada's Governor General; Ishbel, Lady Aberdeen, becomes the first president of the National Council of Women.

William Lyon Mackenzie King

KING AND HIS TIMES

1896
King receives a Bachelor of Laws degree from U of T.

Mrs. Menden, a fortuneteller, accurately prophesies King's future; the U of C again offers him a scholarship to study political economy; he moves to Chicago and briefly moves into Hull-House, where he works as a volunteer.

1897
With the encouragement of Postmaster General William Mulock, a family friend, King studies the sweat shop system; he writes his thesis on the International Typographical Union and receives his Master of Arts from U of T.

1898
King goes to Harvard University and receives a master's degree.

Having met nurse Mathilde Grosset the previous year while recovering from typhoid fever, King contemplates marriage; his family reminds him that his "first duty is to those at home;" he recovers from his love affair while holidaying in Rhode Island where he tutors the sons of a wealthy family and meets Julia Grant, the granddaughter of Ulysses S. Grant.

CANADA AND THE WORLD

1896
Liberal Wilfrid Laurier becomes the first French-speaking Roman Catholic prime minister of Canada; he appoints Clifford Sifton minister of the interior with instructions to encourage immigration to the organized North-West Territories; he appoints William Mulock as postmaster general.

1897
While he is in London attending a colonial conference, Canadian prime minister Wilfrid Laurier is knighted by Queen Victoria.

Ishbel, Lady Aberdeen, founds the Victorian Order of Nurses in Canada.

1898
William Gladstone, former British Liberal prime minister and social reformer, dies.

The Earl of Minto becomes Canada's Governor General.

KING AND HIS TIMES

1899

King completes the oral part of his PhD at Harvard; the university grants him a travelling scholarship, which he uses to go to Britain, France, Switzerland, Germany, and Italy; he receives a telegram in Rome from Mulock offering him the editorship of the new government *Labor Gazette*.

1900

King becomes deputy minister of labour, the youngest in the history of Canada; he brings his expertise to the country-wide unstable labour situation; his friend and roommate, Henry Albert "Bert" Harper, is assistant deputy minister of labour; they have an active social life but also read aloud to each other from the works of Matthew Arnold, William Morris, and Alfred Tennyson.

1901

King begins to travel the country serving on Royal Commissions on Industrial Disputes; returning from British Columbia (B.C.) he gets off the train in Toronto to read in the newspaper that Bert Harper has drowned while trying to rescue a skater on the Ottawa River; King is devastated and is unable to write in his diary for three weeks.

CANADA AND THE WORLD

1900

William Mulock becomes Canada's first minister of labour.

A head tax on Chinese workers entering Canada is raised from $50 (1885) to $100 because of white workers' fears in B.C.; Canada asks Japan to restrict the number of its immigrants.

1901

Theodore Roosevelt becomes the twenty-sixth president of the U.S. when he succeeds William McKinley, who has been assassinated.

1902

The largest boatload of immigrants Canada has ever seen arrives in

Halifax; most of the immigrants are Jewish.

1903
William Mulock is instrumental in connecting Canada and the United Kingdom through the radio.

The Chinese head tax rises to $500 in Canada.

1904
In Canada, J. S. Woodsworth (future politician) moves to Winnipeg, Manitoba, and begins his work at the All-People's Mission with immigrant slum dwellers.

Earl Grey becomes Canada's Governor General.

1905
A statue of Galahad is erected on Wellington Street in Ottawa as a monument to Bert Harper; the inscription, chosen by King, is from Tennyson's *Idylls of the King*: "Galahad... cried, 'If I lose myself, I save myself.'"

King meets Violet Markham, a wealthy British woman with a social conscience.

1906
The Secret of Heroism, King's book about his friend Bert Harper, is published.

1905
The organized North-West Territories in the Canadian west are divided into the provinces of Alberta and Saskatchewan.

KING AND HIS TIMES

1907
King drafts the Industrial Disputes Investigation Act, which is designed to solve disputes between management and labour before strikes occur.

After riots in Vancouver's Japanese quarter, Laurier sends King to B.C. to enquire into Japanese losses and into the larger issue of Asian immigration; Japan agrees to limit emigration; American president Theodore Roosevelt invites King to hear his country's concerns; King goes to Britain to meet with officials in the India and colonial offices; he pleases Laurier when he points out that the Indian Emigration Act forbids Indians to emigrate under contract to work in Canada.

King becomes a Companion of the Order of St. Michael and St. George.

1908
King wins the House of Commons seat for the riding of North Waterloo in Ontario.

1909
Harvard University grants King a PhD.

King becomes the minister of labour in Laurier's cabinet.

CANADA AND THE WORLD

1907
American president Theodore Roosevelt bars Japanese from immigrating to the U.S.

1909
J.S. Woodsworth publishes *Strangers Within Our Gates*, which says that non-English-speaking immigrants are undesirable.

William Lyon Mackenzie King

1910
King and his family vacation at Kingsmere.

1911
The Liberals' loss of the general election means that King's efforts to prevent the incidence of phosphorous necrosis and his bill to prohibit the manufacture, importation, and sale of matches made with white phosphorous is not passed.

Violet Markham offers to provide King with a yearly income.

1911
In the Canadian federal election Robert Borden's Conservatives defeat Laurier's Liberals.

The Duke of Connaught becomes Canada's Governor General.

1913
More than 400,000 immigrants – the largest number in one year – arrive in Canada.

American millionaire John D. Rockefeller, Sr. endows the Rockefeller Foundation, a philanthropic organization that focuses on public health and medical education at first and later supports the sciences, agriculture, and the humanities. His son, John D. Rockefeller, Jr., is elected president of the Foundation.

Coal miners employed by the Colorado Fuel and Iron Company, a Rockefeller interest in Ludlow, Colorado, strike for union recognition.

KING AND HIS TIMES

1914
Unemployed after his electoral defeat and too old to join the army, King seeks work in the U.S.; he becomes director of industrial investigation for the Rockefeller Foundation.

King's hometown of Berlin changes its name to Kitchener.

1915
King visits his brother, Max, who is in Colorado being treated for tuberculosis (TB), and receives the news that his sister, Bella, has died.

King uses his knowledge of labour relations to find a solution to the Ludlow, Colorado strike; he persuades the company and the miners to compromise and accept company unions.

1916
In August, King's father dies.

1917
King takes his invalid mother to Kingsmere for the summer while

CANADA AND THE WORLD

1914
Britain declares war on Germany and Austria-Hungary; as a part of the British Empire, Canada is automatically at war.

The ship *Komogata Maru*, bringing 350 East Indians to work in B.C., is not allowed to land at Vancouver; after two months in the harbour, Canadian warships escort the ship and its passengers out of the harbour.

In Ludlow, Colorado, open warfare ensues between the striking miners and the militia; fourteen people are killed in the "Ludlow Massacre"; federal troops arrive.

1916
The Duke of Devonshire becomes Canada's Governor General.

1917
In France, Canadian soldiers, fighting as a unit for the first time,

William Lyon Mackenzie King

KING AND HIS TIMES	CANADA AND THE WORLD

he works on a book about labour relations; in December she dies in his Ottawa apartment while he is out of town electioneering.

In the "conscription" election, King does not win his seat.

suffer heavy losses but capture Vimy Ridge.

In Canada, Prime Minister Sir Robert Borden prepares a conscription bill, a measure particularly unpopular in Quebec; in August the Military Service Act brings in conscription; Borden becomes leader of the Union government, which is a coalition with Liberals opposed to Laurier's anti-conscription platform; the Wartime Elections Act gives the vote to female relatives of soldiers.

In Russia, the Bolshevik Party seizes power in the October Revolution.

1918
King's book *Industry and Humanity* is published.

1918
In Quebec City, soldiers kill four protesters during anti-conscription riots; the Canada Elections Act gives the vote to all women in federal elections.

The First World War ends on November 11; 60,000 have died and many more are permanently injured.

1919
At the Liberal Party leadership convention in August, King offers to heal the divisions caused by the conscription crisis and to find new solutions to the problems of tariffs, freight rates, labour and the concerns of the newly developing Left; he wins the leadership.

1919
In February, Sir Wilfrid Laurier dies in Ottawa.

The Winnipeg General Strike, which begins on May 15, climaxes on "Bloody Saturday" on June 21.

The first radio broadcasting licence in Canada is issued to

KING AND HIS TIMES

King is elected to represent the riding of Prince in Prince Edward Island.

1921
King runs in his grandfather's old riding of North York in the general election in December and his Liberals win a majority of the seats; he becomes the tenth prime minister of Canada and chooses to serve as minister of external affairs too.

1922
In March, King's brother Max, who is afflicted with muscular dystrophy and TB, dies.

1923
King sends his fisheries minister and Quebec lieutenant, Ernest Lapointe, to Washington to sign the Halibut Treaty, the first treaty

CANADA AND THE WORLD

XWA, an experimental station in Montreal.

1920
Canada is a founding member of the League of Nations; farmers from Ontario and the Prairies unite with dissident Liberals to form the Progressive Party; Borden retires and Arthur Meighen becomes prime minister and leader of the Conservative Party.

Unemployment insurance is introduced in Great Britain and Austria.

1921
Representing the Independent Labour Party, J.S. Woodsworth is elected to the House of Commons where he becomes the "conscience of Canada"; Agnes Macphail is the first woman elected to the Canadian Parliament.

Lord Byng becomes Canada's Governor General.

William Lyon Mackenzie King

independently negotiated and signed by a Canadian government.

King attends the Imperial Conference in London; he is determined that the Dominion of Canada will be more independent.

1925
In the October federal election, King loses his majority and his seat; but the Conservatives do not have a clear majority and so King decides to govern with the support of the Progressives; he asks for a vote of confidence from Parliament.

1925
In Canada, Lady Byng donates the Lady Byng Trophy to the National Hockey League to reward sportsmanship combined with excellence.

King appoints O.D. Skelton undersecretary of state for external affairs; Skelton will become a key adviser on domestic as well as foreign affairs.

1926
King runs in a by-election in Prince Albert, Saskatchewan and wins.

With his support dwindling because of a customs scandal, King asks the Governor General, Lord Byng, to dissolve Parliament; Byng refuses; King resigns; Meighen becomes prime minister on June 29 but quickly loses a vote of confidence and must call a general election.

On September 25, King becomes prime minister again with the help of the Liberal-Progressives; in

1926
Viscount Willingdon succeeds Lord Byng as Governor General of Canada.

Ernest Lapointe leads the Canadian delegation to the Imperial Conference committee chaired by former British prime minister, Lord Balfour, which deliberates on relations between self-governing parts of the British empire.

KING AND HIS TIMES

October he sails for England and another Imperial Conference.

J.S. Woodsworth bargains with King: his vote in return for an old age pension plan; Agnes Macphail of the United Farmers of Ontario Party also supports the plan.

1927
King entertains Charles Lindbergh, who is the honoured guest at Canada's Diamond Jubilee birthday celebrations, which include the dedication of the Carillon in the Peace Tower on Parliament Hill.

King's book *The Message of the Carillon and Other Addresses* is published.

1930
King appoints Cairine Wilson to the Senate; she is the first female senator.

King and Lapointe campaign throughout the West for the general election; although Mrs.

CANADA AND THE WORLD

1927
American Charles Lindbergh flies his monoplane "Spirit of St. Louis" nonstop from New York to Paris in thirty-three and a half hours.

R.B. Bennett becomes the leader of the Conservative Party of Canada.

1928
In Britain, Lord Byng becomes Chief Commissioner of the London Metropolitan Police.

1929
With the collapse of the U.S. Stock Exchange in October, the ten-year-long Great Depression begins.

William Lyon Mackenzie King

KING AND HIS TIMES	CANADA AND THE WORLD
Bleaney, a fortuneteller, promises victory, King is defeated by R.B. Bennett and his Conservatives.	
1931 In June, the Beauharnois Scandal becomes public; Opposition Leader King denies any knowledge of the affair but says it has thrust the Liberals into "the Valley of Humiliation."	**1931** The Statute of Westminster, based on the Balfour Report of 1926, recognizes the autonomy of the self-governing parts of the British Empire – Britain, Canada, South Africa, Australia, New Zealand, and the Irish Free State – and creates the concept of the Commonwealth.
1932 Having met a medium named Etta Wriedt, King invites her to come to Ottawa to conduct a seance with him and his friend Joan Patteson; they believe they are speaking to King's mother and grandfather.	**1932** Fear of another incident like the Beauharnois Scandal prompts the Liberal Party of Canada to create the National Liberal Federation to separate fundraising from the parliamentary leadership.
1933 King and Joan Patteson try to communicate with the dead without going through a medium.	**1933** In Canada, the Co-operative Commonwealth Federation (CCF) is founded under the leadership of J.S. Woodsworth.
	Franklin Delano Roosevelt becomes the thirty-second president of the U.S.
	1934 Mitch Hepburn becomes premier of Ontario.
	The Earl of Aberdeen, former Governor General of Canada, dies; his widow, Ishbel, seeks solace in automatic writing.

KING AND HIS TIMES	CANADA AND THE WORLD

1935

Campaigning on the slogan "It's King or Chaos," the Liberals sweep back into power in the federal election

1935

Two new parties win seats in the Canadian general election: Social Credit and CCF; included among the new MPs is Tommy Douglas, future father of medicare.

Lord Tweedsmuir becomes Canada's Governor General.

1936

King purchases the pillars from a bank building about to be torn down and installs them as an "Arc de Triomphe" at Kingsmere to celebrate his recent successes, which include civic beautification projects in Ottawa, the closing of relief camps, and his work with the League of Nations in Geneva.

1936

The Spanish Civil War begins.

Mussolini and Hitler declare the Rome-Berlin Axis.

Maurice Duplessis and the *Union Nationale* win a landslide victory in the Quebec election.

In Great Britain, King George VI succeeds his brother, Edward VIII, who has abdicated in order to marry the American divorcée Wallis Simpson.

1937

King attends the Imperial Conference and the coronation of King George VI in Britain; he visits Hitler in Berlin and is impressed by the dictator. He predicts that Hitler will deliver his people.

1937

John D. Rockefeller, Sr., founder of the Rockefeller family fortune, dies in Florida.

In Canada, the drought in southern Saskatchewan is the worst in its history; left-wing Canadians volunteer for the international brigades fighting in Spain; the Rowell-Sirois Commission on Dominion-Provincial Relations hears submissions from delegations across the country.

William Lyon Mackenzie King

1938

Hitler marches into Austria; Britain tries to appease Germany at Munich.

1939

In March, King declares that Canada regards any act of aggression against Britain as an act of aggression against the whole Commonwealth; in the same month he promises that "conscription of men for overseas service will not be a necessary or effective step;" in August he is feted by the Liberal Party.

Though his spirits have assured him that Hitler does not want war, King's government declares war on Germany and Italy; in December he signs the document creating the British Commonwealth Air Training Plan.

1939

King George and Queen Elizabeth visit Canada and the U.S.

The Spanish Civil War ends; the Second World War begins in September; the U.S. is officially neutral.

General Andrew G.L. McNaughton becomes commander of the 1st Canadian Infantry Division; he will be the senior Canadian officer in Britain as the force grows to an army by 1942.

Ishbel, Lady Aberdeen, dies.

1940

Mitch Hepburn passes a resolution in the Ontario legislature criticizing King's war effort; King calls an election and wins a huge majority; the Unemployment Insurance Act passes.

The National Resources Mobilization Act introduces conscription for military service within Canada; the men conscripted under the act are sometimes called Zombies.

1940

In Canada, after many unsuccessful attempts, John Diefenbaker wins a seat in the federal election; James L. Ralston becomes the minister of defence and begins to campaign for conscription for overseas service.

The Earl of Athlone becomes Governor General of Canada.

Winston Churchill becomes prime minister of Great Britain.

KING AND HIS TIMES

1941

In his maiden speech in the House of Commons, future Conservative prime minister, John Diefenbaker, taunts King, who happens to be his MP.

Pat, King's dog and companion, dies.

After flying to Britain in a Liberator bomber, a reluctant King addresses the Canadian Corps; he meets with Churchill, who reassures him that conscription for overseas duty will not be necessary.

1942

King continues to consult the spirits with his friend Joan Patteson; he worries about dividing French and English Canadians; Minister of Defence Ralston threatens to resign over conscription; as a compromise King agrees to hold a plebiscite in April to find out if the people of Canada will release him from his promise of no conscription.

1943

The plebiscite having freed King from his promise, he continues to vacillate because Quebec has voted against it; all King's Quebec ministers have promised to oppose conscription; King adopts the motto "Conscription if necessary, but not necessarily conscription."

CANADA AND THE WORLD

1941

In December, Canada declares war on Japan following the Japanese attack on Pearl Harbor; Canadian troops surrender to Japan in Hong Kong a few days later; the U.S. and Canada forcibly move citizens of Japanese descent away from the west coast of the continent.

In Canada, O.D. Skelton and Ernest Lapointe die.

1942

The Allies launch a disastrous attack on the French port of Dieppe; 5,000 Canadian troops are involved, 900 are killed.

In Canada, Progressives and Conservatives link to form the Progressive Conservative Party of Canada; J.S. Woodworth dies in Vancouver.

1943

Canadian infantry and a tank brigade take part in the invasion of Sicily in July; Canadian forces attack Ortona, Italy in December.

General McNaughton resigns from the Canadian army.

William Lyon Mackenzie King

KING AND HIS TIMES

1944
King invites Louis St. Laurent to become minister of justice and attorney general; although he is from Quebec, St. Laurent agrees to support King in whatever measures he thinks are necessary to win the war.

Ralston resigns; retired General McNaughton, a favourite of King's, replaces him as minister of defence; King announces that conscription is now necessary; thousands of Zombies are sent overseas.

1945
Family Allowance legislation having been passed by the King government in the previous year, families with children sixteen years old and under begin to receive the "baby bonus" on July 1.

In San Francisco to work on the draft charter of the United Nations (UN), King hears from his valet that the war is over.

In the general election, the Liberals win a strong majority; King now represents the riding of Glengarry, Ontario.

CANADA AND THE WORLD

1944
Allied forces land on the Normandy beaches of France in the D-Day invasion on June 6; the Canadian army loses 5,000 men in the Battle of Normandy.

President Roosevelt of the U.S. dies and Harry S. Truman succeeds him.

1945
In May, Canadians liberate western Holland; Germany's surrender ends the war in Europe; in September Japan surrenders after atomic bomb attacks on Hiroshima and Nagasaki.

In Britain, family allowances are introduced; Lady Byng publishes *Up the Stream of Time*, which includes a moving tribute to Canada.

Soviet intelligence officer Igor Gouzenko defects and reveals a widespread espionage network operating in Ottawa.

1946
Winston Churchill, no longer prime minister of Britain, gives a

KING AND HIS TIMES	CANADA AND THE WORLD
	speech in the U.S. in which he uses the term "Iron Curtain" to describe the developing Cold War.
1947 The Canadian Citizenship Act, which defines the country's people as Canadian instead of British subjects, comes into force on January 1; King receives certificate 001.	**1947** India is proclaimed independent and is divided into India and Pakistan.
King goes to England for the wedding of Princess Elizabeth; he meets spiritualist Geraldine Cummins.	
1948 On a visit to London, England, a frail King visits his old friend, Violet Markham; when King falls ill, distinguished statesmen visit him at his hotel: King George VI, three prime ministers – Nehru of India, Fraser of New Zealand, and Liaquat Ali Khan of Pakistan – Nehru's sister Madame Pandit of India, and Eric Louw of South Africa. Spiritualist friends whom he has met through Lady Aberdeen also call on King at his hotel.	**1948** General McNaughton becomes Canada's permanent delegate to the UN. The Liberal Party of Canada chooses Louis St. Laurent as its new leader in August.
In April, King becomes the longest-serving elected statesman in the English-speaking world; in July, Joan Patteson informs Violet Markham (Mrs. James Carruthers) of King's weakened condition; on November 15 he retires as leader of the Liberal Party.	

William Lyon Mackenzie King

KING AND HIS TIMES	CANADA AND THE WORLD
	1949 Canada is one of the founders of the North Atlantic Treaty Organization (NATO). Senator Cairine Wilson is Canada's first woman delegate to the UN.
1950 King dies on July 22 at Kingsmere.	**1950** The Korean War begins in June; Canada will send men to support the UN initiative.

Acknowledgments

The author gratefully acknowledges the kindness and assistance of the following people: Bob M. in Picton and the cab-sharing lady in Ottawa; the exceptionally kind and generously helpful Parks Canada staff – Juan Sanchez, Jennifer Drew, Lorenzo Cotroneo, Louise Hamelin, Patrick Ste-Croix, and Bernie Roche at Laurier House National Historic Site; Robert Roe, Carolyn Blackstock, Kathleen Le Faive, Rob Girardin, Kim Seward-Hannam, Diane Paquette at Woodside National Historic Site (one of my favourites); Derek Cooke, who surely must dream about Willie by now, and the gracious Ellen Manchee, Parks Canada Ontario Service Centre; staff of the National Archives of Canada (mille mercis – upstairs and downstairs); University of Chicago Office of the Registrar; Annie Dicaire, Department of National Defence; University of Toronto Archives and Harvard University Archives; Mom-the-Awesome-Editor Goodall and Sheila O'Hearn of the same department; Chris Raible, friend and William Lyon Mackenzie guru; John Cooke of Cooke and Associates, Ottawa; the Parliament Buildings tour guides; the lightning-fast Interlibrary Loans Department staff, Ottawa Public Library; and XYZ Publishing for the opportunity to retell the WLMK story. Thanks everyone for your cheerful help!

Selected Sources

Primary Sources

BYNG, Viscountess Evelyn. *Up the Stream of Time.* Toronto: Macmillan, 1945.

BYNG, Baron. *Correspondence with William Lyon Mackenzie King*, June, 1926. www.nlc-bnc.ca

CANTACUZÈNE, Princess Countess Spéransky née Grant. *My Life Here and There.* New York: Charles Scribner's Sons, 1921.

CUMMINS, Geraldine. *Mind in Life and Death.* London: Aquarian Press, 1956.

House of Commons Debates. Vol. 1, 1923. Vol. IV - V, 1926. Vol. 2, 1930. Ottawa: F. Acland. Vol. VI, 1944. Ottawa: Edmond Clouthier.

KING, William Lyon Mackenzie. *Diaries.* National Archives.

KING, William Lyon Mackenzie. *Industry and Humanity: A Study in the Principles Underlying Industrial Reconstruction.* Toronto: Macmillan, 1935 edition.

KING, William Lyon Mackenzie. "Biographical Sketch and Letter to E.H. Wells, Editor of *The Bulletin*, Harvard University," Ottawa, January 3, 1908.

KING, William Lyon Mackenzie. *The Message of the Carillon and Other Addresses*. Toronto: Macmillan, 1927.

MARKHAM, Violet. *Friendship's Harvest*. London: Max Reinhardt, 1956.

POWER, Charles G. *A Party Politician: The Memoirs of Chubby Power*. Ed. Norman Ward. Toronto: Macmillan, 1966.

Newspapers and Magazines
The Hamilton Spectator
The Kitchener Daily Record
Maclean's
The Ottawa Journal
The Toronto Star
The Vancouver Daily Province

Secondary Sources
Articles and Unpublished Sources
Clipping Files, William Lyon Mackenzie King, Woodside National Historic Site. Grace Schmidt Room, Kitchener Public Library.

MANCHEE, Ellen et al. Interview with Dr. James Gibson, Laurier National Historic Site of Canada, Ottawa, Canada, March 16, 2,000, transcripts and videotapes. Parks Canada, Ontario Service Centre.

MARTIN, Ged. "Mackenzie King, the Medium and the Messages," *British Journal of Canadian Studies*, Vol. 4, 1, 1989, p. 109-135.

PENNEFATHER, R.S. "New Light on John King – a note." Kitchener Public Library.

VYE, Kathy. "King at Laurier House: 1923-1950." Unpublished Study: Canadian Parks Service, Ontario Region Office, 1992.

Books

BERTRAND, Luc. *L'énigmatique Mackenzie King*. Montreal: Les Éditions L'Interligne, 2000.

BOWERING, George. *Egotists and Autocrats: the Prime Ministers of Canada*. Toronto: Penguin, 1999.

COOK, Ramsay. *The Regenerators: Social Criticism in Late Victorian English Canada*. Toronto: University of Toronto Press, 1987 edition.

DAWSON, R. MacGregor. *William Lyon Mackenzie King: A Political Biography*. Vol. 1: 1874-1923. Toronto: University of Toronto Press, 1958.

ESBEREY, Joy. *Knight of the Holy Spirit: A study of William Lyon Mackenzie King*. Toronto: University of Toronto Press, 1980.

FERNS, Henry and Bernard OSTRY. *The Age of Mackenzie King*. Toronto: James Lorimer, 1976.

FRENCH, Doris. *Ishbel and the Empire: A Biography of Lady Aberdeen*. Toronto: Dundurn Press, 1988.

GRANATSTEIN, J.L. *W.L. Mackenzie King*. Don Mills: Fitzhenry and Whiteside, 1976.

GRAY, Charlotte. *Mrs King: The Life and Times of Isabel Mackenzie King*. Toronto: Penguin Books, 1997.

HENDERSON, George. *W.L. Mackenzie King: A Bibliography and Research Guide*. Toronto: University of Toronto Press, 1998.

HUTCHINSON, Bruce. *The Incredible Canadian: A candid portrait of Mackenzie King: his works, his*

times and his nation. Toronto: Longmans, Green
and Company, 1953.

McKENTY, Neil. *Mitch Hepburn.* Toronto: McClelland
and Stewart, 1967.

MOORE, Laurence. *In Search of White Crows:
Spiritualism, Parapsychology, and American
Culture.* New York: Oxford Press, 1977.

NEATBY, Blair H. *Mackenzie King: The Prism of Unity,
1932-29.* Toronto: University of Toronto Press,
1976.

NEATBY, Blair H. *William Lyon Mackenzie King: The
Lonely Heights.* Vol. II, 1924-32. Toronto:
University of Toronto Press, 1963.

NICHOLSON, Murray. *Woodside and the Victorian
Family of John King.* Hull: Minister of Supply and
Services Canada, 1984.

NOLAN, Brian. *King's War.* Toronto: Random House,
1988.

PICKERSGILL, J.W. and D.F. FORESTER. *The Mackenzie
King Record.* Vol. I-IV. Toronto: University of
Toronto Press, 1960-70.

ROAZEN, Paul. *Canada's King.* Oakville: Mosaic Press,
1998.

STACEY, C.P. *A Very Double Life: The Private World of
Mackenzie King.* Toronto: Macmillan, 1977 edition.

TEETER, William. *Mackenzie King: Man of Mission.*
Don Mills: Nelson, 1979.

THOMSON, Dale C. *Louis St. Laurent: Canadian.*
Toronto: Macmillan, 1967.

VON BAYER, Edwina. *Garden of Dreams: Kingsmere
and Mackenzie King.* Toronto: Dundurn Press,
1990.

WHALEN, Dwight. *Mackenzie King's Christmas Letter to a Little Girl*. Niagara Falls: Horseshoe Press, 1992.

Web sites and Film

http://www.archives.ca
http://www.canadianheritage.gc.ca
http://www.canadianheritage.org/reproductions/20962.htm
http://www.cic.gc.ca/english
http://www.civilization.ca/hist/cadeau/cagif02e.html
http://collections.ic.gc.ca
http://www.dfait-maeci.gc.ca/department/history/
http://www.gg.ca
http://www.nlcbnc.ca/primeminister
http://www.nytimes.com/learning/general/onthisday/
http://parkscanada.pch.gc.ca/pm/english/King_e.HTM
http://www.rochester.edu/pr/Review/V61N1/feature3.html
http://www.uic.edu/jaddams/hull/ja_bio.html
Mackenzie King and the Conscription Crisis. National Film Board of Canada, 1991.

Visits

Laurier House National Historic Site of Canada, Ottawa, Ontario.

Mackenzie King Estate, Kingsmere, Quebec.

Parliament Buildings, Ottawa.

Woodside National Historic Site of Canada, Kitchener, Ontario.

Index

Halibut Fisheries Treaty (with
U.S.), 71, 157, 158
Handy (secretary), 127
Harper, Henry Albert (Bert), 21,
35, 37, 39, 40; drowns (1901),
42, 151; 43, 47, 74, 90, 152
Harvard University, 20, 35, 36, 39,
40
Head, Sir Francis Bond
(Lieutenant Governor, Upper
Canada), 71, 145
Heeney, Arnold (secretary, War
Committee), 106
Hepburn, Mitchell (premier of
Ontario), 107, 108, 160, 162
Herridge, Rev., and Mrs. (family
friends), 40, 42
Hitler, Adolf, 97-9, 102, 105, 132,
161, 162
Holland, 130; liberation of, 164
Hull, Cordell (secretary of state,
U.S.), 105
Hull-House, Chicago, 31, 32, 148,
150

Imperial Conferences, (1923), 75,
104, 158; (1926), 79, 104, 158,
159; (1937), 98, 104. 161;
(1948), 133, 135
Independents (Independent
Labour Party), 79, 157
India, 135, 136, 165
Indian immigration to Canada, 44,
45, 153, 155
Industrial Disputes Investigation
Act (1907), 44, 153
Italy, 36, 113, 118, 151, 162, 163

Japanese immigration to Canada,
labour disputes, 44; riot in
Vancouver (1907), 44; intern-
ment in 1941, 163

Kilbasco, Marilyn, 127, 128, 129.
See also Woodside
King, Bombardier John (paternal
grandfather), 8, 144, 145
King, Christina (paternal grandmother), 6
King, Dougall Macdougall (Max,
brother), 4; birth, 147; 10, 16,
17, 28, 41; tuberculosis, 53, 54,
56, 155; muscular dystrophy, 70,
72, 157; death, 73, 74, 157;
after-death communication with
WLMK, 94, 95, 110, 131, 139
King, Isabel, *née* Mackenzie
(mother), x; birth, 146; marriage,
147; 3, 4, 5, 6; plays piano, 7; 8-
11; paints, 12; 16, 28, 31, 34; dis-
approves of Mathilde Grosset,
35, 150; 47-49, 55, 59; suffers
stroke, 60, 61, 155; 62; death,
63, 156; after-death messages to
WLMK, 68, 73, 74, 85, 86, 90-
94, 110, 113, 125, 131, 138, 139;
WLMK's memories of, 64, 69,
70, 72, 142
King, Isabel (Bella, sister), 4; birth,
147; 6, 10, 14, 16-18, 24, 28, 46,
47, 49: death, 54, 155; WLMK's
memories of, and spiritual communication with, 55, 64, 68, 69,
73, 74, 110, 131, 138
King, Janet Lindsey (sister), 4;
birth, 147; 7, 10, 17, 18, 28, 34;
disapproval of Mathilde Grosset
35, 150; 40, 47, 59, 63, 70; Mrs.
Lay, 88
King, John (father), x; birth, 146;
marriage, 147; 3, 5-7, 9-13, 15,
16; Queen's Counsel, 18; 23, 25,
28, 29, 31, 33, 34; disapproval of
Mathilde Grosset, 35, 150; 46,
47, 55, 59; senator, 60; death,
59, 60, 159; after-death presence

Printed in April 2003
at Marc Veilleux imprimeur,
Boucherville (Québec).